When despair for the world grows in me
and I wake in the night at the least sound
in fear of what my life and my children's lives may be,
I go and lie down where the wood drake
rests in his beauty on the water, and the great heron feeds.
I come into the peace of wild things
who do not tax their lives with forethought
of grief. I come into the presence of still water.
And I feel above me the day-blind stars
waiting with their light. For a time
I rest in the grace of the world, and am free.

~Wendell Berry

from
The Peace of Wild Things and Other Poems

First Printing: 2023

ISBN 978-1-7329988-5-8

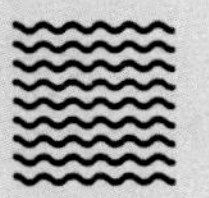

Chesapeake Publication

Chesapeake Publication
1010 Dulaney Valley Road
Towson, MD 21013

www.chesapeakepublication.com
www.heidischreiberpan.com

Edited by
Photo by Payton Schreiber
Illustrations by Sebastian Schreiber-Pan
Typesetting/formatting by Sebastian Schreiber-Pan

Printed in the United States of America

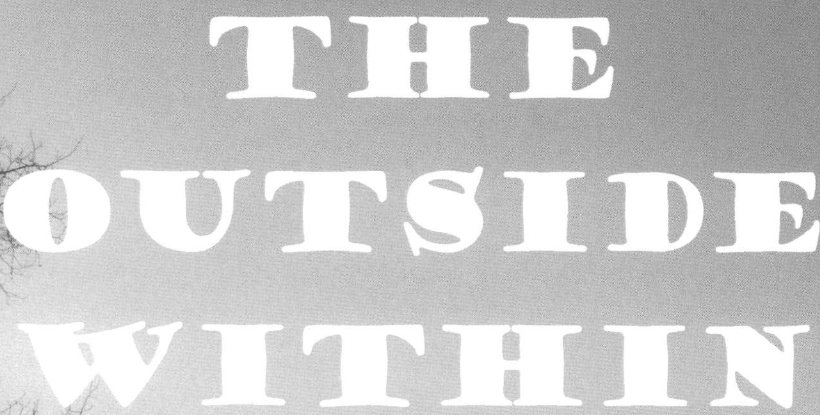

Stories of Nature's Role in Psychological Well-being

Contents

Introduction 7

PART ONE
NATURE AS MIRROR – INTERIOR WILDERNESS

PREFACE: The benefit of self-inquiry for social-emotional wellbeing 12
Heidi Schreiber-Pan

I AM ENOUGH: The healing of self-doubt 14
Dagmar Bohlmann

HEAVIEST BACKPACK: The space between dependence and self-reliance . 22
Zoe Jack

PERMISSION TO ENTER: Navigating access to nature 33
Julie Ayers

ANCESTRAL AWAKENING: Finding myself amidst the ancients 41
Laura Marques Brown

PART TWO
NATURE AS TEACHER – LIFE LESSONS LEARNED

PREFACE: Education of *Homo sapiens* 54
Heidi Schreiber-Pan

BLACK OR WHITE: A zebra's lesson on identity 56
Barney Wilson

AGAINST THE CURRENT: A river instructs on resistance and allowing 64
Gina Strauss

UKULELE SPEAKS: Music and mindfulness on the Appalachian Trail 72
Phillip McKnight

STRETCHING FOR GROWTH: The perks of taking risks outdoors 78
Bryan Gomes

TRUTH IN THE SADDLE: Learning to show up 86
Tracy Sanna

PART THREE
NATURE AS COUNSELOR – FROM SORROW TO SOLACE

PREFACE: The emotional benefit of being attached to nature 12
Heidi Schreiber-Pan

ON EDGE WITH ANXIETY: A green heron leads the way out 98
Brian Rollfinke

A BLADE OF GRASS: Freedom from addiction in the web of life 106
Erin Quinley

NATURE'S MOTHERING: Walking together on a road called grief 112
Kate Gerwin

HUNTING FOR PEACE: A mountain helps with traumatic stress 121
Land Tawney

PART FOUR
NATURE AS SPIRITUAL GUIDE – SACRED CONNECTIONS

PREFACE: The psyche of a spiritually connected human race 132
Heidi Schreiber-Pan

CALL OF THE WILD: An exploration of interspecies sacredness 134
William Homestead

CONCH SHELL CALLING: On a mission to negate nature deprivation 143
Catherine (Missy) Gugerty

HIKING WITH ANGER: An invitation to authenticity 150
Greg Cochran

TOWARDS A WILD GOD: Facing mystery on the threshold 158
Beth Jones

Afterword: Unplugging Generation Z 168

Acknowledgment and Dedication 170

References and Resources 172

Contributors 178

Photo and Artwork Credits 180

About the Editor 181

INTRODUCTION

What is it you plan to do with your one wild and precious life?

~MARY OLIVER

I stared back at him and said, "Just leave me here to die, I can't walk another step." I figured dying was the better alternative to picking up my 60-pound pack and continuing on this trail from hell. My newly wedded husband responded by pulling out the cooking gear to warm up a can of baked beans, then spoon-feeding me while I was laying spread-eagle in the middle of the soaked forest floor.

"I hate hiking. I hate carrying this pack full of wet clothes. I hate this frickin' rainstorm." As the warmth of the beans started to radiate through my body, I noticed the hot sting of tears rolling down my cold face. It had only been two days in the backcountry when a hurricane unexpectedly changed course heading inland toward two young hikers in the Blue Ridge Mountains.

It had started as a fun adventure. A bunch of rookie backpackers invading REI just to realize we couldn't afford 99% of their merchandise. So, we hit the local thrift store and purchased a gigantic pack, big enough to haul half of our household goods. And that is just what we did. Even two cast iron pans made it on the trip, clunking loudly with every step – our homemade bear alert system. Although our packs were bearing down on our shoulders with ferocious strength, we happily embraced the trail ahead.

Then the storm hit. First with a drizzle, then a downpour mixed with hail. I remember how cold my wet cotton shirt felt against my skin.

Now, my husband moved into action, setting the tent up in no time. Eventually, we fell asleep to the gentle sounds of the nearby trickling stream.

"What in God's name is that roaring sound?" I quickly unzipped the tent and glanced outside. The stream had turned into a deafening river, rapidly growing in size and threatening to swallow us up at any moment. "We got to move, hon," I said in sheer panic.

There is something very chaotic about packing up amid a storm. We stuffed all the wet gear into our mega-bags and ran from the bellowing river as fast as our legs would go.

At this point on the loop trail, heading back would have increased our mileage. As a result, we continued uphill, nonetheless. I am someone who can say with all sincerity that I encountered my mental boundary, my limit, my "end-of-the-road" when the wet gear on my back was pulling me to the ground with an intensity of ten burning suns.

Three hours after the bean-feeding session, we stumbled upon a road and hitch-hiked back to our car. Due to the lack of any dry clothes and the need to warm up our bodies, we stripped down, and sat butt-naked in the car, cranking the heat.

Our adventure concluded at a nearby fast-food drive-thru. Hunger pains forced us to think creatively. We awkwardly covered our bodies with old paper road maps and ordered two burgers to go. To this day, I remember the look of incredulity on the drive-thru attendant's face.

With help from nature-as-teacher, I learned at the age of twenty-four that I needed more grit in my life; the skill of pushing through. I looked fine on the outside. But on the inside, I was soft and a slave to my mind's tagline, "I can't tolerate discomfort and pain."

Many more instances of "safe suffering" in the great outdoors have instilled a powerful motivation to achieve perseverance. I understand now that discomfort does not mean danger. That successfully managing discomfort is the best medicine for self-doubt and insecurity.

In a greater sense this book, like my adventure in the Blue Ridge Mountains, illustrates nature's ability to show up in big ways and provide what we need at the moment. In my case it was perseverance, in your case, it may be relaxation and comfort. Astonishingly, nature has a great variety of experiences, lessons, truths, wisdom, and ancient medicine seemingly made to order for each one of us.

The following true accounts enter this narrative as the natural world provides mirroring qualities that enlighten our self-awareness in the best of ways. The more-than-human world is filled with the possibility of delivering solace in hard times as well as sacred meaning-making for the human spiritual journey.

With nature as mirror, teacher, counselor, and spirit guide, this book invites you on an outdoor journey filled with wild promises echoing from our ancient past of deep connection and passionate bonding with our Mother Earth.

I.

NATURE AS MIRROR

INTERIOR WILDERNESS

PREFACE:
The benefit of self-inquiry for social-emotional well-being

"Like water which can mirror the sky and the trees only so long as its surface is undisturbed, the mind can only reflect the true image of the self when it is tranquil and wholly relaxed."

~Indra Devi

In the weeks prior to turning forty, I wasn't sure if grieving or celebrating was the way to mark the occasion. Being known as a rather cheerful person, I opted for rejoicing by gifting myself a nine-day retreat in New Mexico. The purpose of the retreat was to cultivate a connection with nature through silence and outdoor meditation. Nobody bothered me for a week and serenely meditating in the mountains near Taos sounded heavenly.

So often, the fantasy we create in our minds is far from the stark reality of the experience. Here I was, two days into my silent retreat, planning my escape. If only I had a way to get back to the airport...

Transferring from the hustle of running a business in the fast-paced environment of a metropolitan East Coast city to the serene woods of Carson National Forest was too much of a culture shock for my busy mind. But the sudden stillness around me in addition to an empty to-do list shone a light on some unresolved internal elements. It was time to journey inward and explore my interior wilderness.

If we think about the wilderness as an inhospitable region or a neglected area, interior wilderness might refer to a corner of our internal landscape that needs our attention. A past loss for example demands a bit more care-taking. On my journey into silence, an old Ponderosa pine held space as I allowed old grief to wash through me.

Something deeply healing occurs when we include nature in our search for greater self-knowledge and desire to bring about our own emotional wellbeing. The natural world, similar to the mirror in your home, reflects an image of whatever is in front of it. The following stories illustrate how nature sends messages of hope and healing. Our powers and gifts are already present within us; nature simply is the mirror that focuses all the light on areas that lie in the shadows of the critical mind.

What we all have in common is a human need that the stories in Part One highlight: the need for nature's counsel and wisdom to guide us toward social-emotional health and wellbeing. The first step in that journey is understanding that we can rarely think ourselves out of a problem and that what we desire is found in the more-than-human world.

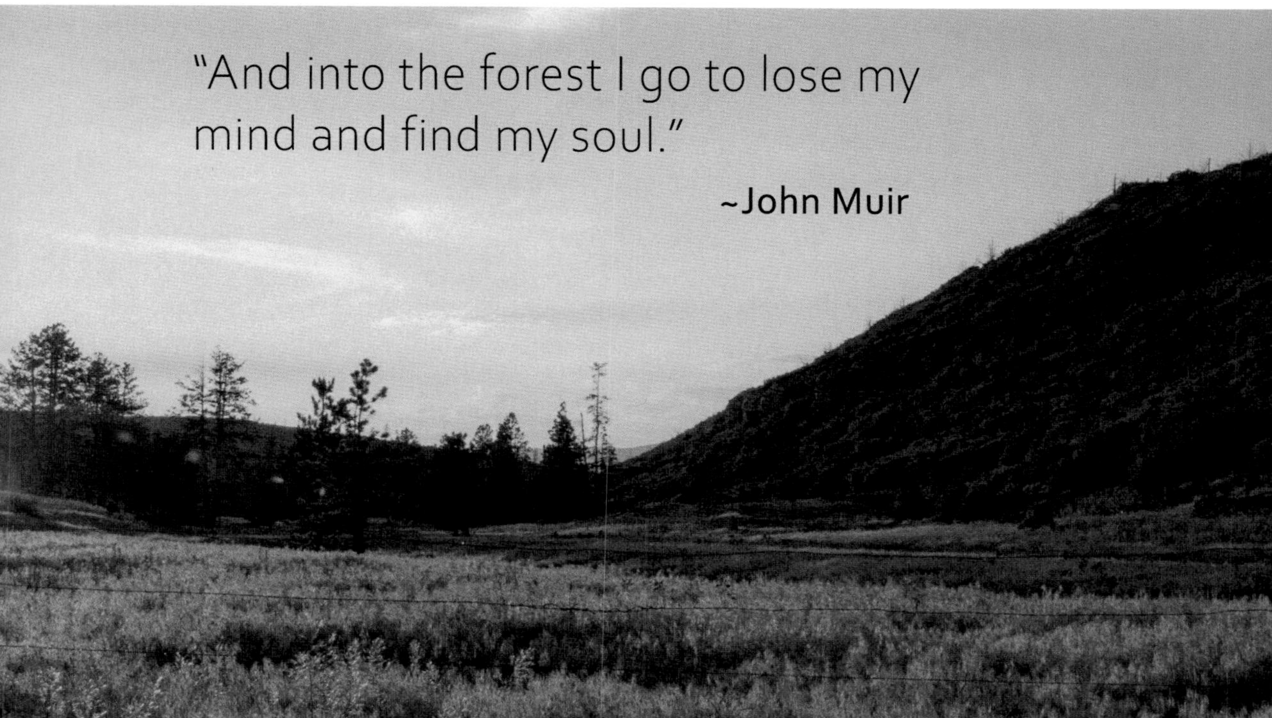

I AM ENOUGH:
The healing of self-doubt

"Nature's peace will flow into you as sunshine flows into trees. The winds will blow their own freshness into you, and the storms their energy, while cares will drop off like autumn leaves."

~John Muir

That's not what I'd say. I'd say it depends on what clothing you wear. I'd say it depends on what the trail conditions are. I'd say it depends on what you have been doing the hour before, the day before, the week before, the year before, the life before. I'd say it depends on if you are walking in pain.

I bet John Muir did not have arthritis, but I do. His fresh sunshine fades into fusty darkness in my body as every step casts shadows of pain. My walks in nature that year before hip surgery became shorter and shorter, and with decreased time in the woods, I noticed sadness creeping in like a noxious weed. As a group fitness leader, I had always associated movement with physical and mental wellness, and this agony was crushing my spirit and my sense of self.

With my identity crumbling like sunbaked dirt, slowly my self-esteem started falling apart. In an indoor cycling class one day, no longer able to rise out of the saddle, sweat turned into tears as I watched footage of my beloved Yosemite National Park on the screen behind the instructor. Would I ever be good enough, fit enough, pain-free enough to hike there again?

The sense of completion after climbing five thousand feet from the Yosemite Valley floor and celebrating the courageous ascent up the majestic granite Half Dome, gripping steel cables with leather gloves like my life depended on it – and it did – left me feeling like I had earned my place in nature. Would I ever be strong enough to meet its dangers and in awe enough to forget blisters and sore legs?

Would I be feeling that sense of wonder again that overcame me when gazing at the clear night sky from a hike-in campsite in Bryce National Park? Seeing millions of stars, I used to be grateful for gravity when my back pressed against my sleeping pad, connecting me to Mother Earth as she spun around herself at one thousand miles per hour. Now gravity describes the significance of my pain better than the forces that hold our world together.

Self-doubt left me feeling disillusioned and disoriented, amplified by our recent move from Tahoe to Maryland for my husband's career. I had stopped teaching yoga, Pilates and cycling so I could focus on settling our son and daughter into middle and high school. But mostly, I just hoped that I could find a way to heal myself. After all, I had spent over twenty years teaching others how to do it. But anyone whose arthritis has eaten away the cartilaginous cushions between bones knows how constantly grinding joints gnaw on your fighting spirit. And while it had always been natural to me to be the cheerleader for others, I could no longer encourage myself to stay positive.

The fight against chronic pain is a very lonely battle you fight quietly on the inside. Even with the support of a chiropractor and a physical therapist, frustration and disappointment gained strength, and my willpower to resist wilted. I used to teach group fitness and ran marathons; now I was riding my bike on a dull rails-to-trails path and felt exhausted. Day by day, I kept losing another part of me. As my connective tissue was wearing out, I increasingly disconnected from the life I used to know. Why is this happening to me? What did I do wrong? I should not have run in that 178-mile relay. Why can't I fix this? Who am I? Where do I belong?

To avoid listening to my grief, I began softly chanting the purifying Gayatri Mantra on my bike rides: "Om Bhur Bhuvah Svaha | Tat Savitu Varenyam | Bargo Devasya Dhimahi | Dhiyo Yo Nah Prachodayat." Professor of religion at the University of Rochester Douglas Brooks translates this mantra as, "The eternal, earth, air, heaven | That glory, that resplendence of the sun | May we contemplate the brilliance of that light | May the sun inspire our minds."

Deepak Chopra, one of my meditation teachers, says that by meditating on the Gayatri Mantra, you will gradually realize the oneness of the whole universe as the radiance of Mother Divine. The mantra is said to remove fear and protect health.

For me, the chant drew my attention into the here and now. But most of all, it changed the way I saw the world and my place in it.

"Instead of seeing nature as a place outside of me or a place to prove myself, I came to appreciate myself as part of the natural world and opened myself up to learning its lessons of change, adaptations, and growth."

As I listened to my voice blending into the symphony of bird songs and waterfalls, I started to appreciate the ordinary moments. I began noticing the particular path the sun found through the canopy to paint patterns on the mossy ground. The sweetness of honeysuckle sometimes stopped me and required another deep inhale. In the pause of savoring these moments of delight, I began to realize how my relationship with nature was changing.

Instead of seeing nature as a place outside of me or a place to prove myself, I came to appreciate myself as part of the natural world and opened myself up to learning its lessons of change, adaptations, and growth. With each breath, I entered this reciprocal relationship: inhaling oxygen from the trees and exhaling carbon dioxide to the trees. With each exhalation came a letting go of my life as it was and a profound acceptance of what it is.

"As this forced slowing down reprogrammed my thinking, nature became my new operating system, one that taught me to be comfortably uncomfortable and perfectly imperfect."

"Pain is not wrong," writes psychologist and meditation teacher Tara Brach in her book Radical Acceptance. "Reacting to pain as wrong initiates the trance of unworthiness. The moment we believe something is wrong, our world shrinks, and we lose ourselves in the effort to combat the pain."

Perhaps it wasn't my arthritis after all, but my attitude that was the biggest cause for my sense of loss. And it seemed as if the simple act of looking up into the tree canopy helped me remember again and again to be hopeful and to experience myself and my life without judging. As this forced slowing down reprogrammed my

thinking, nature became my new operating system, one that taught me to be comfortably uncomfortable and perfectly imperfect. The more time I spent sensing, observing, and noticing the more-than-human world, the more I began to find my inner peace and a deep acceptance of what is. I had gotten all depressed sitting at the kitchen table feeling sorry for myself. But as soon as I went outside, something inside me lifted. It was as if nature around me influenced the nature inside me.

When I finally gathered the courage to schedule total hip replacement surgery, it did no longer feel as if I was giving up, but rather like a yielding similar to a river flowing around an obstacle, like branches, gently swaying with the wind. Perhaps something else wanted to emerge through this experience. Was it possibly the art of accepting?

Post-surgery, confined to my backyard sanatorium for recovery, I started to realize that sitting still with my legs up on my lounge chair no longer equates with being idle, something generally considered not only pointless but sinful in my German family's efficiency playbook. Being in nature helped me filter through my judgments and relax into a joyful patience I had not known before. During this time of forced deceleration, my new mantra became, "I am enough."

While recovering and slowly learning to walk again, first with a walker, then a cane, I became more curious about the research behind nature and healing and soon found fascinating evidence that my experiences were not unusual. Studies show that being in nature will speed the health recovery process, reduce blood pressure, lower cancer risk, and lift people's spirits. Environmental psychologist Roger Ulrich documented in a frequently cited study that even just the view out of a window can accelerate recovery from surgery.

A year later, I had fully recovered and attended a yoga conference in New York where I took a Hiking Yoga workshop. Among the gnarled trunks of American elm in Central Park, I recognized the magical combination of mindfulness and nature. "We are leaving behind the predictability of our rectangular yoga mat in a straight-walled studio and enter the unpredictability of the natural world," said hike leader Eric Kipp. "We build resilience by letting the hiking enhance the yoga and the yoga enhance the hiking."

Convinced that others would equally benefit from combining yoga and hiking, I started YOGAhikes Baltimore together with a friend who, like me, had a twenty-year history of teaching indoors. Based on my own experiences, I wanted people to mindfully soak in the forest's aromas of damp wood and attune to the sounds of crunching leaves leaves and joyful birds. I began to lead participants to rekindle a connection to nature they had lost in their modern, screen-dependent life.

Feeling plush moss and solid granite boulders under their feet, I watched yogis admire the gurgling of a stream while balancing on a rock above it. Out here, moments of childlike wonder and curiosity swiftly replaced attention fatigue and nature deficits. Wanting to learn more, I enrolled in a Mindful Outdoor Leadership course offered at Kripalu, a yoga and Ayurveda retreat center in the Berkshires. Trained in

the Japanese art of forest bathing or shinrin-yoku, I realized that reawakening all senses allows an effortless kind of meditation that is not focused on witnessing thoughts on the inside but rather directing one's focus on nature, offering a stilling of the "turbulences of the mind," as the ancient Indian sage Patanjali called worries and ruminations.

The great outdoors – isn't this the place where all our ancestors spent most of their time? Just a few generations ago, work did not happen behind a screen but out in the green. Today, the Environmental Protection Agency estimates that average Americans spend 90 percent of their lives indoors. Yet, our fascination with the crackling of a fireplace or the rushing of a waterfall signals our deep inner connection to the elements.

My favorite part when camping is lighting the fire in the morning. Waking up with the birds singing their happy good mornings, I love slipping my feet into my UGGs, and noticing fresh morning dew and happy, calm connectivity. With no particular destination other than the firepit, I can be awake in the present moment with full acceptance of who I am, hip replacement and all.

I have fully recovered from my surgery and in fact, had a second hip replaced five years later without the earlier self-doubt or judgment. Instead of losing a part of me, I have found resilience, patience, awe, and wonder through my deepened connection to nature. And with my bionic hips, I have backpacked to the Lost City in Colombia's jungles and climbed the highest mountain in Germany. Instead of seeing myself as a victim of arthritis, a target of my actions, broken and no longer good enough, I feel content. Among the pignut hickory, white oaks, red maples, dogwood, and mulberry bushes that surround my house, I realized that none of them looks like the perfect cotton candy tree I had drawn as a child. Many had broken limbs or stood lopsided but continued to thrive. Here in my backyard, I blend right in with all my imperfections.

In the process of spending time communing with nature, I have also – an unexpected side effect – developed a sense of belonging. And as much as wanderlust still tugs on my shoestrings, I feel content lacing up my hiking boots right where I am to experience the peace John Muir talks about when he sees sunshine flowing into trees. I let the wind blow freshness into me, soak up the energy of storms, drop my cares like autumn leaves, and feel truly blissed by nature.

Radical Acceptance Mantra

While sitting or walking outside, try rhythmically repeating one of the following phrases to practice radical acceptance of a challenging situation. Find a phrase that resonates with you or make up your own. Here are some examples that might help your transition from the stressed flight-or-fight status to a state of ease:

I am that. That I am.

I am rooted. I am alive. I am.

It is what it is.

After every winter comes another spring.

I love and accept myself like a flower loves and accepts sunlight.

Everything in nature happens in perfect timing.

I cannot change the past. I cannot predict the future.

The universe is on my side.

Like the oak inside an acorn, everything I need is already inside of me.

I pause and listen and leave my worries to the wind.

Each insect, amphibian, bird, mammal, each plant, rock, and creek belong here, and so do I.

Earth beneath me. Sky above me. Water within me. Air around me. I am okay.

Like trees that are dropping their leaves, I simply let go.

I delight in the miracles of nature.

The best view comes after the hardest climb.

Acceptance is the answer to all my problems today.

I am enough.

You can also create your own mantra. It is a short positive sentence in the present tense. Some prefer to use phrases from a favorite song or religious text. Buddhist mantras such as "Om mani padme hum" or "So Hum" are often repeated as a calming, grounding, or self-soothing technique.

Repeating a mantra helps the brain untangle from worry and rumination. Simply sit in a comfortable position on the ground or a chair, perhaps leaning against a tree trunk or lying down. Take a few deep breaths, close your eyes if that is tolerable, and begin to repeat the mantra for 5-10 minutes or until you notice a difference in the turbulences of your mind.

Sometimes it helps to handwrite the mantra in a journal and repeat it until the page is full. You could also place it on a sticky note and keep it where you see it often as a reminder throughout your day.

Dagmar Bohlmann

is a registered yoga teacher (eRYT500), a Kripalu certified Mindful Outdoor Guide, and NOLS certified in Wilderness First Aid. She offers powerful nature-based experiences with elements of forest bathing, Ayurveda, meditation, and practical outdoor skills. She is the founder of the popular Maryland-based organization Blissed by Nature. Dagmar has undergraduate and graduate degrees in American Studies from Western Michigan University and the Freie Universität Berlin. She has taught humanities and German at Truckee Meadows Community College in Reno, Nevada, and freelances as a writer and editor.

Heaviest Backpack:

The space between dependence and self-reliance

"A close relationship to nature teaches us that we must never grow too reliant on the group, but that we also must never grow too reliant on ourselves."

~Ralph Waldo Emerson

I was twenty-two years old in the rugged backcountry of Utah when an adolescent boy on the autism spectrum taught me Emerson's true meaning of self-reliance. Growing up on the East Coast in the blinding arms of privilege, I was always fascinated with the concept of what it meant to rely on oneself. As a high schooler at an all-girls prep school, with expectations for my life and opportunities laid out clearly before me, I read Emerson's transcendentalist essay multiple times feeling my skin pulse: 'Trust thyself: every heart vibrates to that iron string. Accept the place the divine providence has found for you… nothing can bring you peace but yourself. Nothing can bring you peace but the triumph of principles." I would curl up in my bed after another day at school having poured every last ounce of my energy into meeting those expectations of others and making the most of those opportunities to find comfort in Emerson's steady words. Nothing can bring you peace but yourself.

I believe it was this relationship with the transcendentalist's essay that laid the foundation for a future year's very important decision. At 22, I chose to leave an esteemed, high-paying job at an international investment firm and packed up my car to live out of it in Utah as a wilderness therapy field guide. Every mile I drove from Baltimore to Salt Lake City, my emotions danced their ferocious pattern between crippling anxiety and enlivening excitement. Trust thyself. Did I trust myself? At the time, the answer was a resounding no, buried under layers of flimsy ego and years of accomplishments that I felt somehow did not belong to me.

A few months into the new job, I had found the new normal. I was working with a group of adolescents, non-neurotypical boys on the autism spectrum. We worked an eight-days-on, six-days-off schedule and co-led excursions into the mountains, deserts, and wildlands across the state of Utah. For the eight-day shift, the other guide, twelve boys, and I became a family: we slept together under one tarp, we ate all our meals in one circle, we crammed into one van to travel to our destinations, we put all our poop in the same tube to be packed out at the end of the trip. Unity among us came quickly in the way that wilderness and forced vulnerability consistently foster.

On one particular excursion, the group headed off to the forests and exposed ridges located on a swath of Bureau of Land Management land east of Provo. Our activity for the week was backpacking. One of the boys in our group, Sam*, was a recent arrival in week three of the program. Even though all the boys had their quirks, his seemed more pronounced. His long, sandy hair was always flopping into his eyes, and while his arms and legs were thin, all of his excess weight gathered around his gut and hips. At the beginning of the excursion, I spent time trying to create a connection with him and learned that his days before wilderness were spent in front of the computer playing video games for hours on end and eating big bags of mini, unwrapped Starbursts that his mother provided. He did not form easy relationships with the other boys or with the guides and soon took on the role of the awkward outcast.

It did not assist his case that on the backpacking excursion, Sam struggled to get his backpack onto his back. Although the packs were large and heavy, the activity of "who will assist Sam in putting on his backpack" soon became a staple in the mornings before we started hiking or at the end of every break for a meal, snack, or water refill. The other boys, especially those who had been in the program the longest, usually took the lead in lifting the pack off the ground while Sam turned his back to them and thrust his skinny arms through. A second or two after the straps were tightened, I held my breath watching Sam totter from foot to foot, anxiously anticipating that one of these times he might just fall over.

I watched this occurrence unfold with great curiosity and mild disturbance. Here we were on a physically demanding backpacking excursion and Sam had not once lifted his backpack onto his back. However, it was not just the physical limits that intrigued me, but also the mental and emotional ones. As the week progressed, it became clear that Sam began to approach these offerings from his group mates with a level of entitlement. And, at the same time, the group had begun to approach their assistance as a baseline expectation, a group norm. As this happened over and over, something inside me began to shift. Nothing can bring you peace but the triumph of principles. If Sam were out here alone, he would not have the physical, mental, and emotional tools to handle his own gear. In many instances in the backcountry of Utah, this would be life-threatening. Were we as guides getting in the way by letting this pattern persist? Were we not doing our jobs?

The job of a wilderness therapy guide is complex and variable. In a ten-day interview and training process, you learn skills from how to make shelter in the treeless desert to what to do when one of your participants tries to run away from camp in the middle of the night. You learn how to stay warm when having to set up camp on twelve inches of snow and how to administer psychotropic medications to your participants while

ensuring they do not pocket the pills in their cheeks to try to take in the future as a large dose. When reflecting on it years later, I realize you only find out what the job is when you start working with the kids. It is then you learn that the job of a wilderness therapy guide is to be a safe and reliable space for a person going through one of the most intense transitions they will ever experience, and nine times out of ten did not choose to experience. And your job, if you are lucky, is to play a role in their growth.

We had been out in the field for about six days when we set up camp on the side of a mountain next to a large teepee assembled from logs. It was morning and the camp was packed up. The boys worked on re-stuffing their sleeping bags and pads, cooking and eating their breakfast of oatmeal or rice and beans, and waited in line to use the space behind the designated "bathroom" tree for that particular campsite. Grey clouds were rolling in over the ridgeline while everyone hoisted their gear onto their backs, and two of the stronger boys lifted Sam's gear onto his. I noticed this as my intuitive churning continued to grow, almost now loud enough to hear. A voice inside of me said, "Today will be the day that Sam will learn to rely on himself."

We filed in a single-file line, doing one last sweep to make sure we had not forgotten anything, and started to walk down the trail. I walked in the back of the pack with Sam and one of the other boys. We talked about the Pokémon card game to pass the time during the beginning of the hike as our brains and bodies awoke. When we emerged from the pines and onto an exposed face on the side of the mountain, I noticed Sam had fallen behind me. The other boy and I, now discussing the evolution of Bulbasaur into Ivysaur, stopped and turned to see what had stopped Sam.

"My shoe was untied!" Sam shouted. The wind was picking up and it was somewhat difficult to hear him. "I had to take off my backpack to tie it. Will you help me put it back on?"

By this time, the rest of the group had trailed ahead. As guides, we carried clunky radios, as well as our cell phones, so it would not be any trouble to reach out to my co-leader and say we were delayed. Our group did not have any specific destination to reach, so time on our feet to cover miles was not a factor. I felt myself standing at a crossroads not only for Sam's growth, but for my own. My mind calculated the facts quickly and responded from the subconscious place that had been building in me for the last six days.

"No. You will put on your backpack yourself."

Sam's mouth dropped open. Compassion and empathy rose in me as I watched him stand there looking at his backpack as if he were intimidated by it. Looking into his eyes, I recalled what it felt like to have the reliable social structure that surrounds you suddenly drop and be standing in front of a challenge alone. In my case, it was voluntary; in Sam's case, it was strongly encouraged. The verbal protests arose in no time. "But I can't!" he exclaimed. "It is heavy, and I haven't been able to lift it this entire trip."

"I believe that you can." I heard the words echo from my mouth. "And, we have nowhere to be, so it is no problem for us to wait here until you figure it out." I sat down on the rock next to the trail. Sam, in his obstinance, also took a seat on a rock next

to his backpack. We were sitting about twenty feet apart as the winds increased and the sky darkened.

Our other groupmate wore an expression of concern on his face. He gestured to me and whispered in my ear, "But it's really no problem. I can go up there now and help him put it on."

I shook my head and whispered back, "No. This is something Sam must figure out for himself."

Within twenty minutes, the other boy got bored and traipsed down the trail to join the rest of the group. Sam was still sitting next to his pack staring at a tree, mulling over the unexpected break in a group norm and its consequences. The clock ticked. 60 minutes. 90 minutes. We both sat on our rocks, reflective and firm in our independent resolutions.

The wind and darkening skies that had been threatening the entire morning soon revealed the meaning of their threats. The sky broke open as chilly rain and medium-sized chunks of ice began spitting onto our heads and backs. I reached into my gear for my rain jacket and yelled up to Sam to do the same. I shifted to another rock under a small bush. Glancing up at Sam, I saw that he looked miserable. It was approaching lunchtime now and his challenge, the backpack, still lay beside him motionless. The emotions Sam had been trying to avoid by relying on help from those around him began to emerge.

"I can't do it!" He screamed. His tears started to mix with the water coming from the skies. He kicked his backpack. "It is too heavy! What am I even doing here?!"

I felt the intensity of Sam's anger and fear float from him to me across the space between us. I scooched further under my bush to avoid the hail as Sam kicked and yelled and experienced agony, a true feeling of defeat. I watched Sam's emotions without comment, without trying to fix them. I let him fully live the fears that were blocking him from even attempting to accomplish this task. I focused my mind on my belief in his capability to change and wrestled with my internal tensions that wanted me to think, "What do you do if he can't lift his pack?" I noticed these thoughts but did not give them power. I remembered similar creeping thoughts as I drove across the country after leaving my high-paying job and going to live out of my car, "What if you can't do it?" I returned repeatedly to my trust in Sam's spirit as I had just recently learned to do with my own.

Soon, the clouds moved through, and the sky calmed. Sam sat back down on the rock, looking at his backpack with different quality in his eyes. I spoke to him from the space under my brush, "What is getting in your way?"

He looked at me no longer with personal anger or resentment, but instead with quiet confidence, and approached his bag. From it, he took one of the long, woven bands that helped to cinch his sleeping bag and wrapped it around the tree in front of him. He pushed and kicked his bag to put it into position behind him and sat down on the ground. Multiple attempts later, Sam engineered his way into sitting on the ground with his backpack on his back and using the band wrapped around the tree to help him pull himself up to stand with his backpack on. Sam walked down the trail proud beaming from behind his shaggy hair, and I greeted him by jumping off the rock, cheering, and giving him a huge hug. At that moment, I recognized a simple fact: There are many places in each of our lives where we have grown to rely too much on the power and influence of others, rather than the power and influence of ourselves. Often though, we need assistance from others to realize what we can do on our own. We cannot make it either entirely on our own or entirely reliant on others. Trust thyself… every heart vibrates to that iron string.

For the rest of the trip, Sam put his backpack on after our stops during hiking. Sometimes his process looked awkward, and he would lose his balance while standing up, but every time he would let the backpack drop to the ground and try again. Initially, the rest of the boys looked at him with perplexity and amusement during his struggles, but over an abbreviated time developed a sense of acceptance and respect for Sam. Sam had faced and succeeded in a journey that the rest of the boys had also taken. In the wilderness, each boy had to combat one or more of the many psychological demons that were in their way. For the rest of our days in the mountains, Sam did not ask anyone for help to put his backpack on.

Self-reliance is a concept that complements human beings' relationship to nature, while at the same time confidently demanding its counterpart, reliance. Sam would not have learned the lesson of his own strength without being a part of the group setting to allow this exploration to occur, just as his initial dependence on the group was impeding him from reaching his potential. In the wake of this experience, I altered my long-term relationship with Emerson's words. A close relationship to nature teaches us that we must never grow too reliant on the group, but that we also must never grow too reliant on ourselves. After all, Sam only was able to learn of his strengths through the safe container that was the assistance of his wilderness therapy family, and that family also had to have the grace to pull back to let Sam explore and grow.

After half a year as a wilderness therapy guide, I traveled back east where I continued to apply this concept of balance between self-reliance and reliance: I try to remain aware of my privilege and where it stops me from venturing out of my comfort zone; I intentionally lean into the places of discomfort to get to know myself a little more; I strive to realize when I have taken on too much myself and need to ask for assistance from others; I seek to stay in a place of awareness, balanced in that delicate space between being dependent of the social web of humanity and being responsible for my piece in it.

> *"Self-reliance is a concept that complements human beings' relationship to nature, while at the same time confidently demanding its counterpart, reliance."*

In my subsequent jobs, activities, and even long hikes, I took what wilderness had taught me and eagerly applied it to maximize day-to-day contentment. Emerson, I agree with you, accept the place the divine providence has found for you. And, I will now add, remember that you are never quite alone.

Developing Self Reliance in Nature

The key concepts that Ralph Waldo Emerson highlights in his writing on self-reliance offer important guidance on becoming more autonomous. Reflect on these four ideas and take note of where you can still improve.

1. Taking responsibility:

"Do I take full ownership of my successes and mistakes?"

No finger-pointing allowed.

2. Being informed about the environment you are in:

"Am I willing to create a lifestyle of continuous learning?"

Being informed means collecting practical information that will improve your life.

3. Knowing your direction and the steps required to reach your goal:

"Are you clear on your life goals and do you regularly reflect on how far you have come to reaching your goals?"

SMART goals are specific, measurable, achievable, relevant, and time-bound.

4. Making autonomous decisions:

"Are you confident in your own decision-making?"

We can consider other opinions, but we do not depend on them.

Journal Prompts: After taking intentional stillness to become grounded, reflect on the following questions in a journal.

- In what areas of my life am I reliant on myself?
- In what areas of my life do I depend too much on the opinions, actions, or perspectives of others?
- If I were out on a backpacking overnight trip alone, what would I be most afraid of?
- What does my fear from the question above indicate about my relationship with myself or my relationships with humanity?

Activity: Based on the reflections above, identify one activity – preferably in nature – that is out of your comfort zone that you will engage in to foster your sense of self and confidence. Put it on the calendar and commit time to engage in this activity. Journal afterward about what you learned about yourself through this activity.

Zoe Jack

is a licensed psychotherapist. She specializes in nature-informed and client-centered work with children, adolescents, and adults. As a former wilderness therapy field guide in Utah and a behavior interventionist at a trauma-informed school in Vermont, Zoe incorporates the teachings of the natural world into her treatment approach with individuals and groups. In 2017, Zoe had the opportunity to thru-hike the 2,190-mile Appalachian Trail from Georgia to Maine, solidifying her therapeutic philosophy that connection and presence lead to meaningful healing and growth.

Permission to Enter:
Navigating access to nature

lessons from birds
do not make me move from this spot
where I can drink my tea
while enjoying birds singing out their day's plans
watch spring flowers budding

if I could make my daunting day's To Do list a melody
instead of wear it like a shackle
make every act a note in this musical
could I too make work beauty
~Julie Ayers

You are gifted a body at birth. The spark that is you, that is separate and different than just flesh and muscle and bone, that some call soul and others call spirit, grows alongside the body that you were gifted. The bodiless part of you cannot help but be influenced by the flesh of you – by the gender, the skin tone, the number and shape of limbs, the way your gifted body moves or does not move, works well or struggles to function in ways compatible with the quality of life or life itself.

I was gifted the body of a female. At birth, I was given a host of nifty pairs – ears, eyes, legs, arms, hands. Everything worked incredibly well. This sturdy body of mine, and germinal spirit, felt most comfortable and energized outdoors, wandering through the woods, swimming in lakes and rivers, snow, and water skiing, climbing trees, and riding bikes. For my first twelve years, my selfness, my budding identity, was linked to how I could exist and interact outside in every extraordinary Minnesota season. Trees felt like best friends. The hollow spot in the lilac bush growing alongside my driveway felt more like a safe home than the tiny Cape Cod where I ate my meals with my volatile flesh-and-blood family.

Inside the painted walls of that house, things were often loud, scary, unpredictable, and sometimes violent. Dishes were thrown as well as insults. Inside the painted walls of that house, I felt small and vulnerable. Outside, standing on the ancient stone that made up the cliffs and hills of my hometown, I felt solid. I felt as strong as bedrock. Nature was my refuge from very turbulent home life. I was comforted by the streams and encouraged by the tall trees. No matter what was happening at home, I knew I could eventually escape back into the woods and lose my self, lose my fear and anxiety, and replace it with a deep sense of peace by sharing time and space with wild honeysuckle. I could always reboot my sense of humor by hanging out with chipmunks.

For those first twelve, formative years, I had this critical outlet. I would use the body I was gifted at birth to grab my bike and ride to the river. But one Friday the 13th, two days after my thirteenth birthday, things took a serious swerve, and I suffered a devastating injury to my right knee that began a change of everything.

I spent months on crutches and in immobilizers and casts. No riding my bike or racing up and down the street on the polyethylene wheels of my pom-pomed skates. No swimming. No hiking. No skiing. No escaping to the woods.

Suddenly, at thirteen, I could no longer move easily and freely. I was stuck, mostly in the house, my scope limited by the pain in my armpits caused by the unyielding wooden tops of my crutches. It was so difficult to negotiate rocky, uneven, sandy, or marshy terrain on crutches or with my leg immobilized that it did not seem worth the effort to get into nature. Outside, during a humid Minnesota summer, my leg would get sweaty and itchy encased in the cast or immobilizer. Outside, other kids were riding their bikes, whooping through the woods, and diving into lakes, and I could not.

Being outside, immersed in nature, was central to who I had been and who I was becoming. My identity was inextricably tied to trees and rushing water and pushing my body to fly across the top of snow and race over the uneven forest floor.

And now, suddenly, I was this incredibly sad girl, sitting on a couch indoors, curtains drawn at her mother's insistence they remain shut to keep our un-airconditioned house cooler. I could not even see the sky or trees or grass.

> *"I had to push myself hard to alter my expectations of what my experiences in and with nature looked like. Nature and I needed to go through a period of renegotiation."*

I struggled with anger and resentment and a tractor-trailer truckload of self-pity. I was envious of everyone who could still do the things I could no longer do. I did not want to ride in a boat and watch other people water ski. I did not want to limp through the woods trailing after friends who were leaping over downed trees. That felt like torture and underscored all I had lost. So, I stuck to the inside. I read. And I got very depressed. Thirteen-year-old girls are good at being depressed, but I really went for the gold. I believed my life had been diminished greatly and had become unrecognizable. My access to the things I loved so much, the woods and lakes and river, had become incredibly restricted physically, and my mental attitude was throwing up even more barriers to getting back outside. If I tried to go into the woods, I quickly degenerated into a nasty mental stew of focusing on all the things I could not now do, how slowly and carefully I had to move, how easy it was for my unstable knee to fail me and leave me to stumble and get injured, how absolutely impossible the act of climbing a tree had now become.

Yet, cutting nature out of my life was not making anything better either. Although the access to the outdoors and my ability to interact with the environment had become incredibly challenging, my need for it remained. Being in the woods had always made me feel calm and safe. Bathing in the shade of the trees, watching a fern frond bend and sway under the weight of a beetle traveling across its surface, and trying to count the minnows swirling by my submerged feet was how I had managed to psychologically survive a turbulent and sometimes violent childhood. Nature was my refuge. It was the soothing, stable shoulder into which I could cry. It was where I found joy. It was the escape, distraction, and promise of better times.

As painful as it was to acknowledge all the things I could no longer do, separating myself from nature was even more painful. I missed the woods and the water and what benefits of nature to help me learn to adapt and accept my new normal, I had become far removed from it.

> *"I had to give myself some time and grace to grieve abilities that were lost, learn to adapt and celebrate what I could do, and find my way back to nature on new terms."*

I had to push myself hard to alter my expectations of what my experiences in and with nature looked like. Nature and I needed to go through a period of renegotiation. I needed to find my way back into the woods, so I had to find a way to accept the new limitations my body now operated under. I needed to overcome the shame I felt because of my need to rely on mobility aids. I was embarrassed to wear a big, clunky knee brace or use a cane or walking stick when I was a teenager. I was self-conscious about how slowly and carefully I had to make my way through the world now.

The journey to acceptance of a life lived differently than I had anticipated was not a quick or easy one. Through my teens and twenties, my body continued to assert its limits as other joints imploded. As far as physical abilities went, things were never, ever going to be as they had been during my first twelve years. As my physical body was now altered, I needed to begin working more intentionally on my psychological well-being and stop fighting, denying, and pretending that eventually my body would heal and become as it had been. I needed to accept and adapt and learn new ways. So, I did. I chose to step back outside. I chose to accept the help I needed, whether that help came in the form of a cane, walking stick, brace, braces, friendly hands to hold, or literal shoulders to lean on.

When I had finally reestablished my footing in the woods, figuratively and literally, my body presented me with a new challenge. When I was in my mid-twenties, I was diagnosed with multiple sclerosis. Now, in addition to hyper-mobile and unstable joints, I had to consider limitations like muscle weakness, fatigue, pain, becoming easily overwhelmed by the heat, and the annoying need for immediate access to a bathroom. Once again, I had to give myself some time and grace to grieve abilities that were lost, learn to adapt, celebrate what I could do, and find my way back to nature on new terms – yet again.

I had fought hard to keep nature and outdoor adventures in my life despite my mounting disabilities, understanding that being active outside was not only a source of fun and distraction, but a critical element for me to maintain a healthy and positive mental attitude regardless of what challenges and heartache life held for me. I had wanted to share the treasure that is nature with my children. I had wanted to offer them the same opportunities that I had experienced to become friends with trees and discover the power and peace offered by a river. I imagined all the family hikes and camping trips we'd take, the trees I'd help my kids climb, the bugs we'd quietly watch crawl across pine needles together, and the forts they would make in lilac bushes. I had hoped my children would have the same opportunities to learn and flourish in nature as I did when I was a child.

"No matter what body you were gifted at birth, or what happened to that body along the way, there is a place for you outside. There is a way for you to be amidst the blue and green and brown and buzzing. There is a way for you to move outward and let nature in."

Yet again, things did not go as I had hoped or planned. Both of my children live with serious health issues. My daughter has a rare, progressive, and life-threatening genetic disorder that makes her medically fragile. She also has intellectual disabilities. My daughter and I have spent decades together living through extended in-patient hospital stays or home confinements as she struggles through illnesses, kidney failure, dialysis, cancer treatment, and kidney transplants. My son is on the autism spectrum and hates being outside where bugs can land on him or where he might get sweaty and dirty. Their health needs have resulted in me needing to redefine my relationship with nature and access.

Here again, the girl who felt most alive and most herself with her hand resting against the rough bark of a tree found herself challenged by access to the environment she loved and needed to maintain her equilibrium and mental health. I began to despair and mourn the loss of even the simplest acts of engaging with nature like taking a stroll through the neighborhood with my children with extra health needs. All the struggles I'd had since I was a teenager, all the adjustments and adaptations I'd made to be able to access nature and benefit from its restorative and healing properties were no longer working.

How do you still share your life with trees and streams if you spend so much of your time in a hospital or treatment rooms and if being outdoors is physically unsafe or psychologically stressful for your family members? Despite the challenges of access, I knew it was critical for my children's mental health, as well as my own, for them to create their relationships with nature.

I had to give myself some time and grace to grieve abilities that were lost, learn to adapt, celebrate what I could do, and find my way back to nature on new terms.

Inspired by a screened porch my brother added to his small farmhouse, we decided to build our own. That could be the place our son would feel safe from bugs and be cooled by a ceiling fan while enjoying the antics of squirrels. It could be the place in which our daughter could spend hours and hours outside listening to the birds sing, feeling the wind brush against her skin, and enjoying the fragrance of blooming lilac while remaining safe from mosquitoes that might be carrying West Nile Virus.

Our porch is not so much a porch but a cathedral to all things green and brown and blue and buzzing and growing and dying and always changing. The porch has served as a launching point to our creativity in discovering other ways to help my children engage with nature, like our recent purchase of a tandem kayak so my daughter can join me on the water. We continue to push ourselves to find new ways our entire family, no matter what health issues or physical challenges we may be experiencing, can benefit from all the healing properties found everywhere in nature.

I had learned from the delicate honeysuckle back when I was a child that there is a place for all things in nature, even the ones that seem most fragile. No matter what body you were gifted at birth, or what happened to that body along the way, there is a place for you outside. There is a way for you to be amidst the blue and green and brown and buzzing. There is a way for you to move outward and let nature in.

Disability, Access, and Nature

No matter your ability level or physical or psychological challenges, there are ways to engage with nature.

- Start small and set reasonable expectations so you and/or your family members can build confidence about being outdoors.

- Stop fighting truths. My son hates being outside because of bugs. We needed to stop trying to get him outside and instead figure out ways to help him comfortably access nature in other ways, like on a screened porch.

- Focus on your and your family members' abilities and strengths and explore how those abilities can translate into experiences in nature, for example:

    - Use a tandem bike or kayak

    - Hike with a companion using mobility aids (walking sticks, braces, cane with a seat so you can rest, etc.)

    - Purchase a screen gazebo tent or build a screened porch so even people with outdoor aversions can benefit from being outside while safe from bugs and sun.

- Even when it is impossible to get outside, you can bring nature, and its associated joy and wonder, inside. My daughter and I would create paper flowers that we attached to string and would tuck up in the ceiling tiles of her hospital room to create a floating garden.

Planning is key when you are headed out on an outdoor adventure while dealing with physical challenges. But do not fool yourself that you can plan your way to perfection. Good enough is good enough. Some things to consider are:

Hydration and nutrition needs

Cooling aids like cooling cloths or vests

Sunscreen and bug spray

Medication doses that may be needed while out

Adaptive equipment and mobility aids available that can make things easier and more enjoyable

Selecting parks, sites, and trails to visit that have bathrooms and/or accessible bathrooms. We even purchased a camp toilet to bring along on our adventures.

Bringing along a hammock to string between trees to take breaks and rest if needed

Julie Ayers

is the appreciative and captivated mother to her two adult children with disabilities. She recently retired after a 30-year career with the Maryland State Department of Education where she engaged youth in service to the community so they could grow intellectually, socially, emotionally, and civically. She was the MSDE's service-learning specialist and authored publications on service-learning, an experiential learning strategy, and presented nationally on the topic. Julie has undergraduate and graduate degrees in Journalism and English and American Literature from the University of Wisconsin-Madison. She has taught humanities and writing courses at the Florida Institute of Technology and Loyola College of Maryland. Whenever she can, Julie writes poetry and fiction and goes outside to visit with trees.

Ancestral Awakening:
Finding myself amidst the ancients

Shapes and Forms
The smooth red walls circulating within
Ravens dark as night nesting above
Each call echoing the internal depths
The spirit of the land, impregnated
with existence across time and space
A reminder of humans and more than human beings
who are still here
I walked at a speed where
I could feel my bones touch the clay
Where the click clack was the rhythm of the beat,
and the drum aligned with the natural cycle of night and day

~Roz Katonah

For two weeks our path was the dried-up riverbed that weaved through Southern Paiute, Pueblo, Hopi, Acoma, Zuni, and Ute lands, known today as White Canyon, Utah. What began as a narrow valley slowly transformed into a deep gorge. As we dropped into the canyon, layers of time became exposed, and my perspective began to shift. The earth was deep red and granulated, and after one day it coated every inch of my skin and belongings. The soil was dry, crackled, and resilient from centuries of drought and flood cycles. We traversed the valley during a drought season and were lucky to avoid the dangers of flash flooding in the desert of the American Southwest. Animal tracks and scat gave notice of coyote, fox, rabbit, mountain lion, raccoon, and scorpion.

Ancient cryptobiotic soil was speckled around the landscape, and Ponderosa pines lined the dried riverbed showing us the path where the water once ran.

I was on this journey with my graduate school cohort as part of our training to become nature-based therapists. The fourteen-day backcountry section of our curriculum was intended to serve as an intensive where we would learn how the rhythms of the natural world affect our minds, bodies, and emotions over time. The canyon section served as one of the many rites of passage I experienced during my three-year training, and it offered me insight into how future clients may be impacted by prolonged, physically taxing, and remote experiences outside.

Although I walked as part of a larger group, I often felt alone. As one of two bi-cultural/racial people in my cohort, I noticed quickly that the way I wanted to commune with the land looked differently than many of the white bodies around me. As I traveled across this sacred territory, the farther from other people I felt, the more aligned with myself and my ancestors I became. There was an energetic presence to the land that at times felt overwhelming. Being away from modern life offered me a transpersonal shift, seeing beyond the tangible and physical realm, and feeling into the spiritual and ethereal one. And it was here, in this liminal space, that life became slower, magical, and intense. Through sensation and breath, I was in direct contact with the presence of each moment.

By the time we came upon the first ancestral Puebloan ruins, my body had slowed down and synchronized with circadian rhythms. My breath was steady, even, and earth-bound. I had been waking up with the sun and the chirps of desert birds for a week. The song of the canyon wren and red-tailed hawk were my new alarm clock. Every bit of nourishment I ate or drank was metabolized as fuel for my next step. Nothing went to waste. I fell asleep stretched out under the moon each night, sometimes howling to coax her to rise. This change in scenery and pace offered respite for my parasympathetic nervous system, and the recuperation it needed to truly rest and digest. Our frenetic daily life often blinds us to these important rhythms and connections, especially if we were not raised to value spending time outside each day. I was grateful to have dropped into myself again, to feel connected to each movement again, to be aware of each thought, and to be present with the breath that I often forget is there.

Scientist and researcher David Strayer and his colleagues Paul and Ruth Ann Atchley from the University of Kansas researched why and how this physical recalibration occurs when we have deep immersive nature experiences. Their research found that after three uninterrupted days in nature, "You start to notice things a little bit, to unwind from the modern world. You notice cloud patterns, sounds, and smells, and it becomes acute. You do not need a watch anymore. You forget what day of the week it is." Strayer continues, "If you can disconnect and experience being in the moment for two or three days, it seems to produce a difference in qualitative thinking."

As I experienced this shift in qualitative thinking, I simultaneously noticed a difference in feeling as well. As we walked this ancient path, crossing over arrowheads, bits of dried-up cornhusks, pictograph markings, and remnants of dwellings where families once lived, I felt strong sensations that our group was not alone in those canyons. I began to contemplate my families' nature story and my lineage. Here in this slowed space, the ceremony of my own intergenerational healing began.

I often felt called to sing as we walked, only to hear my voice echo for miles. There were times I would wail to the walls and be witnessed in my wailing like some strange creature during bone-deep transformation. I wanted to commune, stoke the fire of ceremony and be with those who came before me. I wanted to honor them and recognize their presence, to celebrate them. I had never felt so called to be in song. I returned to speaking my first language of Portuguese to communicate, "I see you. I feel you. You are still here." And in a way, I was saying these things to myself, too. "I see myself. I feel myself. I am so awake, alive, and present." I felt so intertwined with this land.

As a first-generation American from a Brazilian family, I was born balancing myself between two worlds. In one world, I speak English and the goal is to assimilate, fit in, speak well, accomplish goals, contain emotion, present well, and keep a respectable and previously agreed upon distance from other bodies. In the other world, I speak Portuguese and the goal is to connect, feed self and others, communicate gratitude and empathy, take up physical space, sing, dance, and feel intensely. In this world, bodies commune closely,

and physical touch is a language that often means, "I love you and I care deeply about you." I value both of my identities today. And as a nature-informed trauma therapist, I have learned that who we are raised by, what foods we eat, what soil we play on, what color our skin is, the historical trauma our bodies carry, what languages we speak, and how we are taught to move or not move, informs how we interact with and impact the natural world. The field of nature therapy, also known as ecotherapy or ecopsychology further recognizes that our internal environment is connected to our external environment.

I was raised to be in tune with nature's cycles, rhythms, and resources and this influences the way I value nature's role in my life today. When the moon is full, I often feel emotionally satiated, sensitive, and tired. When she is new, I am reinvigorated, driven, and open. The seasons can be very reflective of my internal emotional and energetic states of being. In the winter months, I seek slower processes connected to reflection and some solitude, and I physically and metaphorically "go inside." The spring and summer months are often emblematic of abundance and energy when I feel more called to create, collaborate and move my body. As I reflect on my childhood experiences and cultural identity, this intrinsic connection to nature is present.

When my diaper needed to be changed as a baby, I was not cleaned with wipes, but rather held under a running faucet where water rinsed my bare bottom and nourished my skin. This is a cultural norm and ancestral water wisdom that has been passed down between generations of Brazilian women in my family. This is likely where my delight in playing in the water was born.

Similarly, instead of being covered in thick layers of sunscreen and clothing on a hot summer day, as a child, I was encouraged to be naked on the beach and to let my skin breathe. My family believed in the importance of the sun's vitamins for building a strong immune system. As a result, babies in my family were often breastfed in the sun, a medicinal gesture offered from mother to child. I can hear my mother's voice today encouraging me to put my own son "in the sun." Some of my favorite memories in my family are grounded in the traditional Brazilian Churrasco where I am reminded of specific noises, smells, movements, and connections, always occurring outdoors.

While my family did their best to remain connected to natural rhythms and cycles, we have all experienced a collective severance from natural rhythms due to the influences of industrialization, colonization, and modernization. Throughout the field of ecopsychology, this collective disconnect is referred to as the "original trauma." There are two major consequences of this trauma. One is the collective suffering of the human species and the degradation of our overall health. The other is the devaluation and therefore demise of the natural world.

As a nature-informed therapist, it is my deep belief that this original trauma presents in every clinical evaluation session with a new client. They do not have to be conscious of it or able to name it directly for the negative effects to be present: increased reports of addiction or addictive behaviors, increased symptoms of dissociation, depression, anxiety, persistent negative thinking, feelings of isolation, and increased hyper- or hypoarousal responses, trauma reactions commonly called fight, flight, freeze, and fawn. For most of my life, I was unaware of the negative implications that this systemic rupture from nature had. Before I decided to dedicate my life to understanding these implications, I minimized some of my own dis-ease, degradation, and dysregulation. It was not until I intentionally re-immersed myself into the human-nature story, that I realized how unwell parts of me had truly been.

There has never been a more relevant time to be a nature-informed therapist. The year 2020 forced people back outside. The Covid-19 pandemic created a global crisis and in turn, a global pause. We were not able to ignore the world outside so easily because the activities keeping us distracted from it changed, halted, or disappeared entirely. As I transitioned from working in person with clients to seeing them virtually, the focus and course of treatment changed as well. At first, I doubted my ability to do nature therapy online. As it turns out, it became more easily accessible for people, more creative, and much less glorified or romantic. I often asked clients to consider that now more than ever, nature had something to teach us about being interconnected, part of a larger ecosystem, and therefore not at all alone. Nature therapy interventions meant having lunch in the backyard, at a neighborhood park, or with a local tree. Ultimately, the work was focused on the observation of reliable cycles in nature. Paying attention to these cycles helped people feel more grounded during what relationship expert Ester Perele described as "prolonged uncertainty." This exercise of daily immersion, attention, and meditation in nature kept me grounded as well. I would have not been able to sustain helping others during the Covid-19 pandemic without constantly tending to my human-nature resources.

One client's experience with nature remains close to me. In the summer of 2021 when the United States was experiencing some ease in travel and social distancing restrictions, she had the opportunity to attend her brother's wedding. One night while sitting on a beach with her mother, she experienced a moment that she would later need to process in a virtual therapy session. We would come to name this moment a transpersonal (or spiritual/religious/awe-inspiring) moment in nature. The client described the experience of witnessing an unexplainable light travel across a rock formation in front of her with such precision and in such a particular moment that it was overwhelming and consequential. At this moment, she was addressing traumatic childhood experiences with her mother; an act of courage that took many months of preparation and therapeutic work. She walked away from this experience feeling a closer relationship not only with her mother but with her personal belief in a "God". It was a reparative moment because she expressed feeling a shift from scarcity into abundance, faith, and hope. Hope that she could take a leap of faith and be supported, seen, and understood. This reconnection to herself, to her family, and to a higher power was a pivotal moment in this client's healing journey and one that remains proof of the unimaginable magic that can occur when we notice the more-than-human world around us.

Years before the pandemic hit, I had experienced similar transpersonal healing in those red Puebloan canyons. And similarly, the experience initially overwhelmed me. Later that overwhelm transformed into a stabilizing element in my life: a trust that the natural world reconnects us to ourselves, our ancestors, and each other.

Awakened by a plump moon one night in the canyons, with the rest of the cohort sleeping, I lay mesmerized by the dark sky above me. I did not know stars could look like that, but the desert dark zone brought new meaning to the term stargazing.

As I lay there, I slowly began to hear a woman's voice careen down the canyon. there were no words, just an eerie, faint, whispering song of someone trying to make contact. It repeated four or five times, softly and slowly. Each melody was drawn out. At first, my body was constricted with fear. I felt my hands grip the top of my sleeping bag and pull the fabric up towards my chin as I lay there breathless. I could not believe what I was hearing. But as her voice continued to echo down the valley, an unexplainable calm came over me. My breath returned and I smiled. It felt as though my efforts were recognized, and my ancestors were responding to my earlier ceremonial calls by saying, "I see you, too." What had started as a fearful experience, evolved into a moment of nourishment and love.

Cultivating a Connection with Nature

This practice is an invitation to get curious about your personal nature story while cultivating a connection with nature. It is also a simple grounding technique that can be used if you ever feel the need for emotional, physical, or mental regulation. This practice can occur outside or indoors. If you do this practice indoors, you might want to face an open window or get close to a meaningful nature object such as a houseplant you love, an altar of earth materials, herbs, or any natural elements sacred to your culture or lineage. You can have a journal with you for reflection, or you can simply bring yourself and let nature lead the way.

1. Find a comfortable place to sit or lay, supported by nature. You might lean against a tree, lay in the grass, or simply sit in a chair inside and feel the breeze, sun, or rain coming through your window.

2. Close your eyes if that feels okay.

3. Spend the next 5 minutes arriving in your body through deep, diaphragmatic breathing.

4. If you are outside: Put a hand on your belly and a hand on the earth. Inhale through your nose and feel your belly rise (chest remains still). Exhale and feel your belly fall (chest remains still). Your thoughts will wander. Bring your awareness back to the inhale and exhale of your breath and notice if you can start to feel the earth breathing with you.

   If you are inside: Put a hand on your belly and a hand on your chest. Inhale through your nose and feel your belly rise (chest remains still). Exhale and feel your belly fall (chest remains still). Your thoughts will wander. Bring your awareness back to the inhale and exhale of your breath.

5. Once you feel connected to your natural breathing rhythm, imagine a memory in your childhood where you felt closely connected to the natural world. Notice what arises in terms of sensations in your body and thoughts in your mind. Also, notice any impulses you must change, shift, or alter the experience you are in. Connect with this imagery for as long as you like.

6. Take some deep breaths before you come out of this space. Gently blink your eyes open when you feel ready.

7. If you want to reflect or journal about this practice here are questions to consider:

    - How old were you in your childhood memory?
    - Who was with you?
    - Did you feel alone or connected?
    - Were elders, lineage, culture, or traditions visited?
    - Did any messages (direct or indirect) about nature's value come up?
    - How did you feel before this practice?
    - How do you feel now?
    - Did you notice nature sounds and sensations around you while you were reflecting on your memory? Did you notice a connection around you when you "dropped into" yourself?
    - Did you stop breathing?

Practice daily or whenever you need a reminder that you are never alone.

Laura Marques Brown

is an Ecotherapist working in the unceded territory and tidewaters of the Piscataway, Nanticoke, and Susquehannock Nations, known more commonly as Maryland. She is passionate about helping people heal complex and transgenerational trauma through the powerful human-nature relationship. She is equally as passionate about decolonizing the field of Ecotherapy and returning the wisdom of this ancient way of being back to QTBIPOC communities. Laura spends her time as a therapist, consultant and public speaker, helping others learn about how systems of oppression can impact a whole community's sense of wellness and wholeness. Her approach to this work is built on the belief that our identities impact how we relate to the world around us, including how we relate to the natural world. Laura enjoys spending time in nature with her husband and children, growing food in her garden, she loves therapeutically working with horses and goats, and feels an ancestral connection to the ocean.

II.

NATURE AS TEACHER

LIFE LESSONS LEARNED

PREFACE:

Education of *Homo sapiens* - The good, the bad, and the hopeful

There is something magical about sitting around a campfire. It seems to slow down time, allowing each person to step out of the rat race long enough to be enticed by the meditative dance of colorful flames. As the burning wood tames our occupied minds, meaningful conversations often take place around the fire pit. Humans gathering around a flame is far more ancient than anything modern-day living can offer. "The campfire is a forge for ideas. A place to share our experiences, to talk, to laugh, to cry, to deliberate over our challenges and share our success," write evolutionary biologists Heather Heying and Bret Weinstein. "We have used it to make light and create warmth, to increase the nutritional value of food, and to keep predators at bay." Just as the campfire presents the best possible classroom, nature as a whole has permanently taught us lessons not only about surviving but also about how to thrive on this planet.

Humans have evolved over millions of years under the vigilant guidance of nature. Our fragile bodies have been shaped by the earth's changing chemistry. Our minds continue to be hardwired to accommodate stories of endurance and survival. Our spirit is drawn to bodies of water, desert dunes, and the largeness of trees for the felt sense of awe and wonderment.

"Yet, as humans have begun migrating during the industrial revolution to the inside of concrete buildings, nature's ability to impart wisdom has diminished."

The education of *Homo sapiens* has been going on for a long time. Yet, as humans have begun migrating during the Industrial Revolution to the inside of concrete buildings, nature's ability to impart wisdom has diminished. According to the American Academy of Child and Adolescent Psychiatry, children ages 8-12 spend 4-6 hours a day watching or using screens, and teens spend up to nine hours. There is a new teacher in town now and their name is Technology. Though Tech may be an engaging teacher, our mental and physical health is protesting this new way of learning.

On an eight-day backpacking trip in Yellowstone with the National Outdoor Leadership School, I acquired the skills to navigate the outdoors safely and with confidence. More importantly, I learned that being cold and hungry are signs of discomfort rather than real dangers. The wilds of Wyoming taught me more than any other teacher about my ability to tolerate distress and my internal reservoir of resilience. I discovered that I really can carry 50 pounds on my back, I really can make a fire in six inches of snow, and I really can move about grizzly country safely and securely. I really can live simply and lack nothing.

"I really can live simply and lack nothing."

The subsequent stories draw attention to natural teachers which come in curious and unexpected ways. Life lessons are taught by a zebra, a river, a long-distance trail, the Smokey Mountains, and a herd of horses.

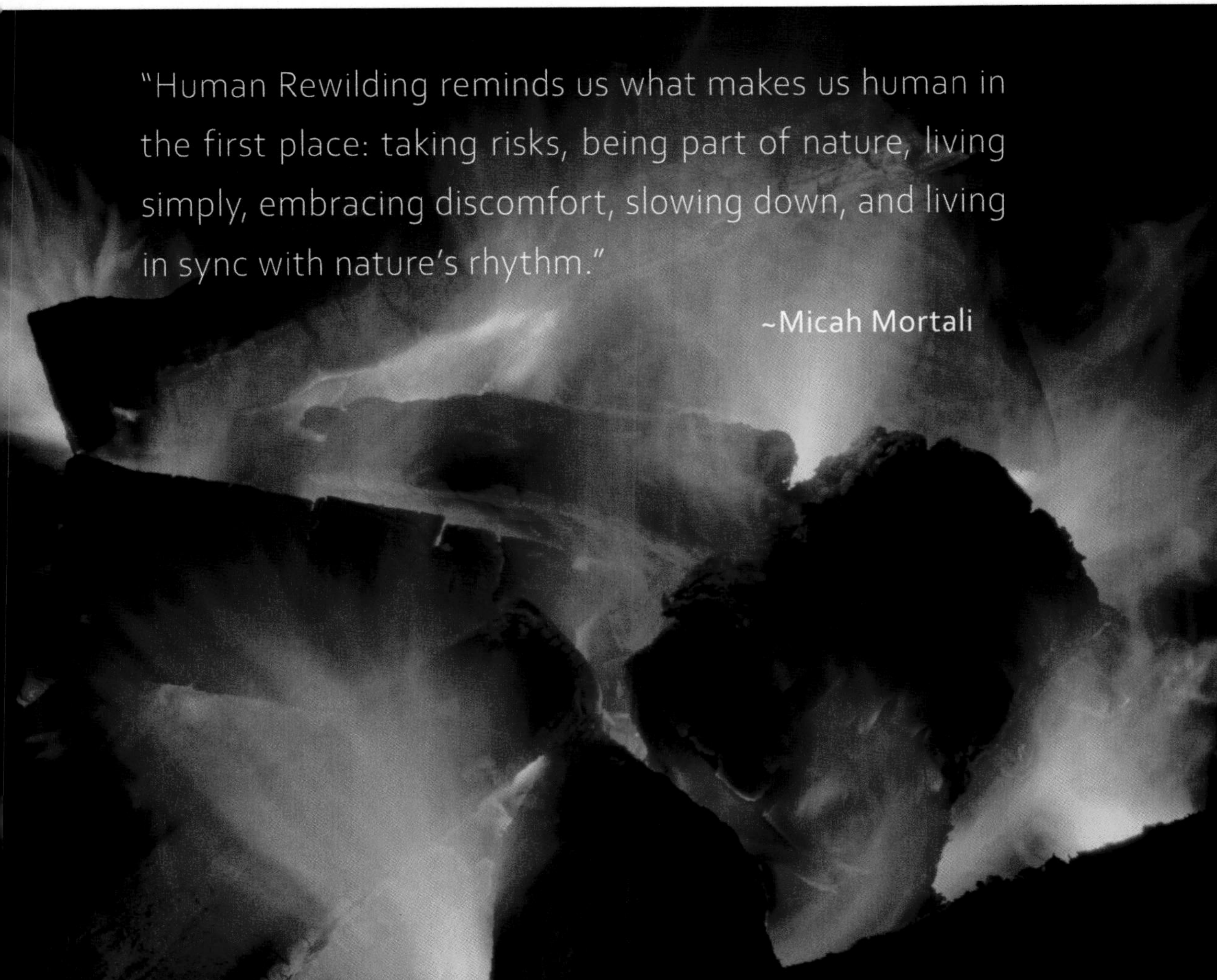

Black or White:
A zebra's lesson on identity

There is a Native American proverb:
"Hin-mah-too-yah-lat-kekt."
It means,
"Every animal knows more than you do."

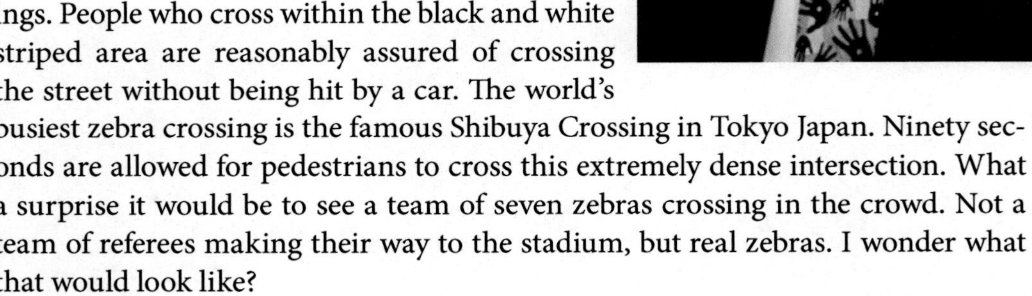

In many countries, busy traffic intersections are made safe for pedestrians by zebra crossings. People who cross within the black and white striped area are reasonably assured of crossing the street without being hit by a car. The world's busiest zebra crossing is the famous Shibuya Crossing in Tokyo Japan. Ninety seconds are allowed for pedestrians to cross this extremely dense intersection. What a surprise it would be to see a team of seven zebras crossing in the crowd. Not a team of referees making their way to the stadium, but real zebras. I wonder what that would look like?

To no one's surprise, those zebras would stand out. It would be amazing, dazzling, and photo-worthy. If posted on social media, the video would quickly go viral. A group of zebras is called a dazzle. That is really an appropriate description of zebras and their behavior. They are strong muscular animals and are classified along with horses and mules as equines. Although no one talks about eating zebras, the meat from their hindquarters is very lean and is said to be sweeter than beef.

My fascination with zebras started when I was a child. I was struck by the way that they look. Their appearance exudes strength and character. They are hard to ignore because of the spectacle of their black and white coats. In a world where most things are seen as either being black or white, I was always mesmerized by the term and wondered, "How do they see themselves? Do they feel stuck between two cultures? How is their self-esteem? How do they cope? Are they aware of their appearance? Are they happy? As a person who sometimes struggles with my self-identity, I knew that if I could answer these questions, I would better understand myself and how to navigate this world.

The neighborhood that I grew up in was unusually tough. There was violence, drugs, fights, and confusion. My family did not quite fit the norm: we had a mother and father in our household. My dad was a police officer, and my mother was a nurse. We were middle class within the African American community. My parents scraped together enough money to send their seven children to the local Catholic elementary school, while all the other neighborhood children went to the dilapidated public schools. Ironically, the neighborhood respected families like ours and held high expectations for us, although we were often teased. We felt like we were not black enough.

As a child, I had very few interactions with people who were not Black. There were multiple White store owners (mostly Jewish), insurance agents, police officers, and priests sprinkled throughout our community. Occasionally, we would see Asians; they owned the carryout restaurants. Black families saw all these people as the untouchable providers of goods and services for our community. We bought from them, interacted politely with them, and life went on. They carried the titles of Mr. and Mrs.

During my teenage years, my interactions with diverse cultures increased both in school and at work. I got a job as a busboy in a very reputable restaurant. I loved the job. The customers at this restaurant were White. I obsessed over eavesdropping on their conversations to understand how they interacted with each other. When they came to the restaurant, I recognized some of their children. They attended the same high school as I. I studied their body language, family dynamics, and decision-making processes. They were significantly different from my family. I often pondered, "How can their lives be so complex?" I had to make sense of these differences.

When I turned seventeen, I was promoted to the catering team, where I found myself in the houses of these same affluent White people. I came face to face with the way they lived and the things they were able to do. It was a far cry from my family's reality. This made clearer the serious inequities of wealth and opportunities between Black and White people.

"How am I supposed to cope? Why don't I have what they have? Why? Why? Why?" At school, I learned that I could excel in a diverse environment and maintain my own identity. I adapted to the environment, performed well, and became one of the top student government officers. My successes led to more questions: "Was I destined to work and live in more affluent environments? Would that require me to shed my Blackness to fit in and advance?" I was perplexed.

Am I a striped zebra? How long would I continue to feel that I was straddling two very different worlds? These internal dialogues accompanied me every day. Like zebras studying their environment, I had to figure out how to succeed with species that were not like me. Zebras coexist peacefully with wildebeest, giraffes, and impalas. Likewise, there are groups of people that I naturally get along with. We spend quality time together, have the same values, and share a common code. We enjoy the sun and the shade in harmony.

"How long would I continue to feel that I was straddling two very different worlds? These internal dialogues accompanied me every day. Like zebras studying their environment, I had to figure out how to succeed with species that were not like me."

Throughout college and my professional life, I remind myself to "think like a zebra" when facing complex issues. I channel my inner zebra to find a way forward that is neither black nor white. The zebra-me is astute, mindful, and calm. It is the superpower that helps me to reach win-win decisions that benefit everyone.

"I channel my inner zebra to find a way forward that is neither black nor white. The zebra-me is astute, mindful, and calm. It is the superpower that helps me to reach win-win decisions that benefit everyone."

I journeyed to Kenya to learn more about myself and to study zebras in their natural habitat. Safaris in The Amboseli, Tsavo National Park, and Maisa Mara provided close-up encounters with zebras. Minutes into the first safari, our jeep approached a dazzle of zebras crossing a dirt road. Wow! A real-life zebra crossing! As we crept towards them, I noticed that the zebras were lined up single file to cross the road. Five already crossed the road and about forty more were waiting. After concluding that our jeep was not a threat to them, the remaining zebras crossed the road one by one. It was calm and orderly.

On the second day of the safari, the guide took us in search of the mighty lion. We drove around the park for about an hour before we arrived where a lion was.

In wonder and awe, we spotted the big boss, the king. We kept still as our jeep quietly crept closer. Our guide pointed out that the nearby zebras and gazelles were frozen stiff in their stances. When lions are near, animals stop what they are doing out of respect and fear for the king of the jungle.

There was so much to learn from that experience. Fortunately, I am now the big boss at work. There are over eight hundred employees in my organization. The company has four locations. When I arrive at each worksite, the signal seems to go out that the lion is sauntering. Workers tense up and are no longer themselves. The pain that I felt when I saw zebras freeze up in the presence of the lion has heightened my commitment to mindfulness in my workplace. I flashback to how I felt as a child when the White police officer walked the beat in my neighborhood. How we learned to know where he was and to track his movement. I remember how relieved we were when he turned the corner and left our block.

At work and in my social environments, there are times when I cannot hide my lifelong developed identity. Although I navigate like a lion; I react in extreme situations with the sensitivity and astuteness of a zebra. I rely on instinct and calmness to proceed. At times, the waters are murky. Like the animals in nature, we deal with our realities and summon our animal spirit to make it through.

The Mara River is a crocodile-filled death trap for most animals that attempt to cross it. It runs between Tanzania and Kenya in the Masai Mara/ Serengeti ecosystem. Unfortunately for the animals in that region, it is directly in their migration path. Each year over two million wildebeest and two hundred thousand zebras and gazelles travel over 1,800 miles in search of rain and ripened grass. They must cross the Mara River in the process. Crossing that river requires guts, planning, communications, good instinct, and luck.

The number of animals that die crossing the river is overwhelming. Proportionally, zebras have a higher survival rate than the other river crossers. Wildebeest do not fare as well. The name used to describe a group of wildebeest is very appropriate: they are called a confusion. They die in numbers because they are everything that a zebra is not. The wildebeest jump into the Mara River in total confusion in an attempt to make a mad dash for the other side. They splash, make noises, and do not look out for each other. It is every wildebeest for himself. They become a smorgasbord for the crafty crocodiles.

Zebras use a different approach. After studying the environment, zebras line up and enter the water at the safest place to cross. They create a zebra crossing. They look for signs of danger and communicate with each other. One by one and equally spaced, they cross. If by chance a crocodile appears, they signal each other and turn back. They are patient and calm. They avoid danger and are not too proud to walk away. They patiently regroup and chart a different path. When each one crosses safely, the others celebrate. Unlike the wildebeest, zebras are tactful and smart. They are truly dazzling.

As I begin to wind down my work-life, I find myself working and living in Africa. It is a dream come true for me as a Black man who has always been in search of my roots and where I fit in. I have a natural comfort level living and working here. The local people have given me the name "Adewole." It means "the Crown has come home." On most days, I feel like I belong. Like a zebra crossing in the famous Shibuya Crossing, I was destined to my natural habitat. I guess the lesson that I learned in this lifelong journey is that you fit in where you fit in. It is not a matter of being comfortable all the time. Sometimes you must be a lion, even when you are really a zebra. And it is ok to have multiple identities. It is what it is. Love the skin that you are in but work on knowing your "inner-most-you."

To Know Yourself, Look to Nature, Look to Animals

Native Americans and other Indigenous people celebrate animal wisdom. Animal spirits can represent confidence, hope, fear, and pessimism. Spend the time to gain understanding from animals and if you are wise, learn to respect and learn from the more-than-human world. Perhaps nature can even teach you about yourself.

The great Spanish writer Miguel de Cervantes said, "Make it thy business to know thyself, which is the most difficult lesson." There are answers in faraway places. Some of these places already live within you. Get out there and find yourself.

Nature, who am I?

For some folks, like me, it takes a lifetime to understand who you are and where you fit in. Spending time in nature, and reflecting on who we are at this moment in time, can bring clarity or solidify our direction in life.

- Find something in nature that embodies your identity in some way. Perhaps, look for objects in nature that represent different parts of you. Arrange the chosen objects in front of you. What do you notice? What theme arises?
- Consider finding elements of nature that correspond to your

  Strengths *Dreams*
  Relationships *Passions*
  Values
- When introducing myself to nature, how would I describe myself. What is my story?
- What natural landscapes do I seek out? Why?
- What animal(s) am I drawn to? How am I like that animal?
- Journal about an interaction with nature/animal that stands out. What did you learn about yourself through that interaction?

"Everyone has a story of animals. Everyone has had some unique experience with them. Sometimes they are domestic animals. Sometimes wild. Sometimes painful and sometimes wonderful. Everyone has been touched by animals in some way, either in life or in dreams, and always the difficulty is determining what it means."

Ted Andrews, author of *Animal-Wise: The spirit language and signs of nature*

Dr. Barney J. Wilson

is an educational leader and entrepreneur currently living and working in Nigeria. He received his doctoral degree in Community College Leadership and Urban Educational Leadership from Morgan State University and his MBA from Carnegie Mellon University. He travels extensively in search of a greater understanding of order, meaning, and mindfulness. This quest has made him a better global leader in helping to reshape and modernize culture worldwide

Against the Current:
A river instructs on resistance and allowing

A woman in harmony with her spirit is like a river flowing. She goes where she will without pretense and arrives at her destination prepared to be herself and only herself.

~Maya Angelou

"Help me, I am stuck under the raft!" The words were there in my head, but I could not speak them aloud because I was underwater. The fun, exciting, white water rafting trip on the Youghiogheny River had taken a scary turn as midway through one of the class four rapids, our raft got stuck, staying suspended sideways on a rock, before dumping several of its occupants out, including me. As the raft passed over my head, I felt the water rushing all around me. I struggled to come to the surface. When my head finally popped out of the water, I gulped in a huge breath of oxygen before I went back under. After doing this a few times, the water began to get calmer, and my lifejacket did its job. I remembered the safety talk before the trip and lifted my feet to keep them from getting lodged between the rocks on the bed of the river. I caught a glimpse of our raft, now floating in the quieter water past the rapid. Our guide was steering the raft over to me quickly, shouting words of support, "Keep your feet up! I am coming! Hold tight!" As he pulled my body into the raft, waves of gratitude flowed through me. I was safe.

Fifteen years later, my husband and I brought our two daughters to the Potomac River in Harper's Ferry for a white-water tubing trip. It was a gorgeous day, and we were excited to have some family time doing one of our favorite things, spending time out in nature. After the bus ride, we carried our tubes down to the river's edge. My husband and daughters climbed in immediately, laughing as the cold water touched their skin. I felt myself hesitate as I looked out over the great expanse of the river. Shaking the feeling away, I nervously climbed in, too.

As I watched my younger daughter Brooke struggle a bit to reach her arms into the water to steer, that feeling of nervousness returned. Flashes of my trip on the Youghiogheny moved through my head. I knew that this was a much different type of trip, however, right away I began to envision the worst.

> *"How many times as a parent have I projected my own fearful or challenging memories onto my daughter's present experience? My fears for her safety connect to my safety concerns. My hopes for her success connect to my dreams."*

Even though Brooke was confident and content floating on her tube, I kept close to her during the entire trip downstream. I even gave her the rope attached to my tube to hold onto for part of it. At one point, hooked together, we both got stuck in a small rapid for what seemed like forever. In actuality, it was only a few seconds. In that short period, I was transported back to those moments of terror on the Youghiogheny River, and I became completely unglued. I scrambled about trying to free our tubes. I shouted directions at Brooke, and she yelled back at me trying to figure out what I wanted her to do. Her previously relaxed state turned into one of panic.

Quickly, our tubes moved through the rapid and we were casually floating down the river again. Brooke stared at me with confusion in her eyes. She had been okay. She knew that she could manage the rapid. It was me bringing my past fearful experience into the now moment that caused the chaos. Brooke looked over at me and said, "Mom, you just freaked me out! I did not know what you wanted me to do." Bam! At that moment, her words figuratively brought me to my knees. Why was I reacting so extremely to a situation that was not, in hindsight, dangerous at all? The last thing that I wanted to do was take away her sense of enjoyment and inner knowing. I said with embarrassment, "I am so sorry. I won't do it again."

How many times as a parent have I projected my own fearful or challenging memories onto my daughter's present experience? My fears for her safety connect to my safety concerns. My hopes for her success connect to my dreams. Wanting to hold her close, not only for her sake but so that I will not have to feel the pain, too.

Anxiety-laced parenting experiences were not new to me. This desire to protect my daughters started the moment they were born. Throughout their childhood, I did my best to keep them safe—physically and emotionally. I bought electrical outlet covers, required them to wear bike helmets, taught them how to use the stove carefully, and provided an empathetic ear when they shared how they were feeling. I bought helpful books and talked with other parents about the best ways to navigate the parenting journey with more ease. As time has gone on, I have realized that being aware of and reflecting on my emotional reactions is the best parenting skill I have.

I remember when my older daughter, Maya, first got her driver's license. My mind was filled with images of auto accidents. I found myself highly attuned to the stories in the news or told by friends that confirmed my fears. Each time she left the house, I would shout, "Please be careful driving!" Or if it was raining, "Remember you need to go slower to have

time to stop!" One day, after months of these well-meaning reminders, Maya stopped on her way out of the door, turned to me, and replied slowly and surely, "Mom, I know. I got this." It took time and several occasions of keeping my hand over my mouth, but eventually, I stopped reminding her and instead remembered that supporting her confidence was more important than any driving suggestion I could offer.

It takes time to develop our present moment awareness muscles. It also takes courage and self-compassion to be able to look in the mirror to see what our children's lives are reflecting back to us. As we continued floating down the river, I watched how relaxed Brooke was in her tube, leaning back, fully stretched out like a lizard basking in the sun. I noticed how tight I was holding my body and felt a pang of envy at her ability to trust so easily. Just as I was asking myself how I could begin to let go of the anxiety that had settled in me, I saw that we were almost at the end of the ride. When we came to our exit point and took our tubes out of the river, the staff at the tubing company told us that we had time to take a second trip. Since everyone else seemed excited about the opportunity, I stifled the "no!" that was bubbling up, and we climbed back into the bus.

During the ride back to the drop-off point, I decided to reflect more on what had just happened. I kept my eyes focused out the window of the bus, taking in the passing trees and riverbank. There was a palpable serenity to them, much different than the uneasiness I was feeling in my body. I began to breathe more deeply as I connected to the strength and stability of the scene. This land was timeless; this river and these trees had been here for lifetimes and would still be here for ages to come. Like my beautifully wise daughter already knew, I was supported by this river and so was she. I could trust the flow, knowing that I had everything I needed to navigate what came my way. I was safely held. In realizing this, my heart began to calm, and I felt my shoulders soften.

We reached the drop-off spot and walked down to the river again. Along the way, I felt the soil underneath my feet and connected again to the energy of the trees. As if by perfect timing, I saw a family of ducks carelessly floating down the river. It was at that moment that I made a conscious choice to set myself and my daughter free.

I was the first one into the river this time. I laid back in my tube and let the sun hit my face. The warmth I felt was exhilarating. Feeling more and more relaxed, I flipped over to lay on my stomach, bringing back my childhood memories of going down the slide headfirst. Inspired, I found ways to spin my tube in circles, laughing at the joy of it. In the quieter moments of my voyage downriver, I admired the passing trees, thanking them for sharing their wisdom. I breathed more deeply than I had for days, taking in the sensations of my relaxed body.

As we climbed out of the water at the end of our ride, we were all laughing and sharing stories. As I listened to Brooke talk about her experience on the river, I noticed the hint of pride on her face for having navigated the river on her own. I felt that same touch of pride in myself as I recognized that, in a moment of mindfulness, I was able to change the quality of my thinking. This, in turn, created a whole new experience for both my daughter and me.

How to Journey from Resistance to Allowing

Living mindfully in the present moment can help to ease those past and future fears. Nature is an incredible support in keeping us in the here and now. The trees, the lakes, and the animals hold space for us to connect to ourselves and remind us that we are a part of a larger world. Sometimes simply sitting in nature can help seemingly large problems return to a manageable size.

Lucky for me, I was given a second chance. With mindfulness and a concentration on my senses, I connected to my surroundings and began to notice all the things I had missed on the first trip through. I connected with my childlike sense of wonder and began to bring joy into the experience. When thoughts of fear popped back into my mind, I breathed through them. I floated down the river with a deep sense of gratitude for the beauty and inspiration that nature was reflecting on me.

The movement to mindful allowing

- Focus on your senses: What do you see? Do you notice any sounds? Are there any smells you can pick up in the air? Find something sensual to touch–a flower petal, a smooth rock, the bark of a tree. Let this information from your senses bring you to this moment.

- Imagine you are a young child. Is there a way to bring to the situation a sense of lightheartedness, curiosity, or childlike innocence?

- When you feel uncomfortable emotions bubbling up, breathe and allow them to move through you. Remind yourself that you can navigate the rapids.

Mindful allowing starts with being present

- Find a place to sit in nature for ten minutes and observe what you see, perhaps even naming your observations aloud.
- Place your hands on a tree. Feel its grounding energy and allow all thoughts of fear or worry to be sent down through its roots into the Earth.
- Look for animals that come into your path and ask them to give you a message of love and support.

Gina Strauss

has worked for over twenty-five years as an advisor, counselor, and teacher in a variety of educational settings with children, adolescents, and adults. She is an advocate for conscious living and believes that much can be learned from life's day-to-day moments. As a certified nature-informed therapist, Gina uses the wisdom of nature to enhance her growth and healing and inspires others to do the same.

UKULELE SPEAKS:
The power of music and mindfulness on the Appalachian Trail

When I hear music, I fear no danger. I am invulnerable. I see no foe. I'm related to the earliest of times, and to the latest.

~Henry David Thoreau

This was my life: waking up, checking my phone, making coffee, breakfast, rushing to work, sitting in front of a computer, quick lunch, more screen time, rush hour, dinner, bed. Repeat. This predictable, stressed-out, fast-paced American lifestyle made me feel numb, and one day, I decided I could not take it anymore. I needed a change.

So, I set out with an out-of-shape body an overweight backpack, and my ukulele to tackle more than two thousand miles between Maine and Georgia. I wanted the Appalachian Trail to test my limits and reconnect me to the rhythm of the natural world. I hoped to reawaken my senses, rediscover my love for music, and open myself up for an adventure.

Soon, I found a new daily routine. Most days, I woke up at five o'clock and instead of reaching for my phone to check messages, I meditated in my sleeping bag. On my way to heat water on a cookstove, I would stop to stretch. I savored three oatmeal packs for a typical breakfast, packed lunch, stuffed my backpack, and by seven o'clock I started walking. For lunch, I would find a spot with a view or by a creek, nosh on dried meat, nuts, cheese, and bread, and continue hiking until six o'clock. The evening chores concluded the day by pitching the tent, collecting water, taking a quick dip to rinse off the day, eating a simple instant backpacker meal, brushing my teeth and after reading a book, crashing on my sleeping pad by eight o'clock.

Slowly, I started to notice the details of life around me. Before sunrise, I sat up in my tent and curiously paid attention to my body sensations. I noticed how my breath merged with songs of early morning birds and the snoring of tired fellow hikers. This daily process of paying attention entuned me with what I was feeling, seeing, and believing. Perhaps I noticed an owl camouflaged in a tree because I had trained my mind to be curious and always ask, "What's happening at this moment?"

In addition to a formal meditation practice every morning, I got in the habit of pausing to reconnect with the moment at every stream crossing and mountain vista. I remember talking with a fellow hiker who was feeling burned out from being on the trail for five months. "I'm ashamed to admit it," she said, "but I don't even stop at any of the vistas. I am just trying to get to the end." Training myself to pause was a vital skill I applied to enjoy the journey, rather than hoping for a projected destination. It also helped me overcome fear.

One day, I carried my empty water bottles down a steep trail, following an old wooden sign that said 'Spring.' Sore from walking up and down the mountains, tired and dehydrated, I was on autopilot. I took a step and suddenly heard a sound coming from near my right foot. I looked and realized I had almost stepped on a timber rattlesnake.

Slowly, I noticed fear diminishing as the sounds of bubbling water increased. I heard birds and let the mountain stream flow over my feet. The fight/flight response faded and made room for a sense of calm and clarity. I realized that fear was there to protect me. The snake was also feeling fear and simply wanted to protect itself from harm. At this moment, I felt a kinship and an honor to connect to a timber rattlesnake, whose population numbers are declining. I wondered what other lessons the snake had to impart.

I had set out on the adventure because I felt stuck in my regular life. Perhaps the snake wanted to remind me to shed old skins. I had a long list of things I didn't like about myself and a long list of stories that weren't helping me be my best self. For example, I did not like my fear of socializing. Turns out, my ukulele would take care of that.

I carried my ukulele around my neck so I had access to music at any moment I felt like playing. I allowed musical ideas to flow out of me as they arose.

In Tennessee, I passed two older female day hikers who asked if I would play the Tennessee Waltz. Even though I did not know the song by heart, I gave it a try, and when I looked up at the end of the song, one of the ladies was crying. In fact, throughout the two thousand miles of walking, five more people teared up when hearing the music I shared. What is it about music and nature and deep emotion? Is it that music gives a safe place for memories to surface? I wonder if the same emotions would emerge had we been in the city, or if we would have even met at all. Perhaps, nature's ability to create safe vulnerability allowed people to open to the healing powers of music.

In addition, a study from the University of Kansas found that people who were immersed in nature through backpacking improved creative thinking and problem solving by fifty percent. The findings point to nature allowing our prefrontal cortex, the part of the brain that assists with accomplishing tasks, to rest and allow creativity to flourish. On the trail, I would sing about how I was feeling to name and accept my current experience which was particularly therapeutic during the times when I was walking alone.

I miss the lifestyle of hiking the AT, specifically the communal feel. It was so natural to stop and talk with a stranger and perhaps even share food. What an amazing way to break down the barriers that I had put up. The experience of intentionally combining mindfulness, nature, and music allowed me to experience inner and outer connections. I was able to understand the workings of my mind and emotions and thus was able to show up more effectively for others.

Bare feet touch the earth
I sit quiet now and see
What I've missed so long

Haiku written on the trail

A Soundscape for Restoration

Making music goes back at least 35,000 years, and the connection between music and nature is ancient. Anthropologists believe that the origin of music was inspired by early humans trying to imitate bird songs. Birds use a strikingly similar rhythmic structure and combination of notes found in human-made melodies.

Like a landscape that contains various landforms, trees, buildings, or other visual stimuli, a soundscape encompasses all the sounds available to you. Our nervous system usually reacts pleasantly to natural environments where manufactured sounds are not dominant.

Soundscape Inquiry

- What soundscapes create inner calm for you?
- Science has shown that the sound of water, birds, and gentle wind is particularly relaxing. How can you integrate these sounds into your daily life?

Research at Stanford University has demonstrated that "listening to music seems to be able to change brain functioning to the same extent as medication," stating that music is an easily accessible and effective stress reduction tool.

Music that reduces stress

Native American flute

Celtic string or flute

East Indian stringed instruments

Music itself can serve as a meditation tool if one is committed to paying attention to the sounds without multitasking.

Playlist for mental wellness

- Streaming music can be a form of self-care
- In 2020, streaming platforms saw a rise in playlists named "calm" or "self-care"
- What songs elicit positive emotions?
- What songs help you relax?
- Are there certain songs that inspire coping skills?
- Create your personal playlist that helps you power down or picks you up
- Consider expanding your interests and looking into binaural beats, singing bowls, or attending a sound bath.

Phillip McKnight

is trained in the Mindfulness Meditation Teacher Certification Program by Tara Brach and Jack Kornfield. He currently works as a mindfulness coach with individuals and various organizations including schools and health care institutions. Phillip has worked as a naturalist, educator, community advocate, and guide for groups such as The Audubon Society and the Chesapeake Bay Foundation. He combines his skills in mindfulness and environmental leadership, as a mindfulness teacher with the Center for Nature Informed Therapy in Baltimore, Maryland.

Stretching for Growth:
The perks of taking risks outdoors

We cannot escape fear. We can only transform it into a companion that accompanies us on all our exciting adventures. Take a risk a day, one small or bold stroke, that will make you feel great once you have done it.

~Susan Jeffers

Do you know your physical limitations? Do you really? How do you know? Or rather, how do you think you know? Do you remember the first time you rode your bike without training wheels – or doing something you were not completely comfortable with at first? Of those things you have now done more than a couple of times – do they feel different? How so?

Each March, I find myself in the Smoky Mountains leading a group of high school students. For over ten years, I have been working on this backcountry wilderness expedition that continually proves to be an outstanding way to build character in these soon-to-be adults. Groups are prepped and educated on the Outward Bound-style expedition and what safety precautions need to be reviewed for several weeks ahead of departure. When they arrive in the wilderness, somewhere along the Tennessee and North Carolina border, they are split into crews with two adults and one student leader. Each person carries both group and personal gear in their backpacks that weigh 50-60 pounds.

It was about day three of our trip traveling on single-track trails over rolling hills and through thick woods lined with rhododendrons and mountain laurel. After a couple of days of observing our six students, I was impressed with how they were working together, learning navigation skills, and displaying some early leadership. A couple of our students seemed to have extra trail stamina because they were student-athletes. Unfortunately, it was these two boys that got our crew into a jam later that day. With seven miles to go, a drizzle and a cool temperature, we reminded our students to have their rain gear on or at least easily accessible. About an hour later, the rain had stayed light but steady, we caught up to our students who were hiking slightly ahead of us on the trail.

They had stopped to look at their maps and compasses to get oriented in the woods. We noticed that our two student-athletes had not put on their rain gear while other students had rainproofed and even added layers for warmth. It was an effort to convince them of the necessity of staying warm and dry. Two hours had passed when we again caught up to them on a snack break. The rain had slightly increased, and the air temperature was now about 50 degrees.

Checking in with the two boys, I noticed they were a little lethargic compared to their usual selves. One of them was showing the effects of the wet and cold. Their core body temperature seemed low and had to be coerced into putting on a hat and gloves.

As the students put on their backpacks to finish the last couple of miles to our evening's campsite in the woods, I noticed Jack had some dexterity issues and could not open the zipper of his backpack. He seemed a little surprised, frustrated, and confused. Consequently, I walked directly behind him as he was now the slowest hiker of the crew. Observing his body language, I noticed him stumbling and staggering a bit in addition to having trouble carrying his backpack. He had a glazed look in his eyes, and I realized I needed to stay in close contact with him until we got to our campsite for the evening. The other students and leaders began to hike ahead with the rest of the crew. The two of us proceeded at a slow and painful pace. Within no time, it became clear that I would need to carry his pack to keep us on track. I was leapfrogging him, carrying my pack for one hundred yards, and then dropping it and going back and carrying his for a little

while. An hour later, when we finally arrived at our site for the evening, the other student John was borderline hypothermic. It was now dusk, the rain had picked up, and within five minutes of each other, both students started to shake uncontrollably and with chattering teeth they were unable to speak in full sentences. I realized it was time for my Wilderness First Responder training to go into effect as we needed to get them out of their wet clothes.

As the rest of the students got visibly upset, we had our student leader take them to a separate area so we could get the two students in need under a tarp shelter and into dry clothes and sleeping bags to do rapid warming. At this point, the students had lost motor skills and were violently shaking. It was a scary scene, but it was a previously practiced first-aid scenario.

After about twenty minutes both students warmed up and reached homeostasis. One student even fell asleep and started snoring loudly. The other mentioned feeling hungry and asked for a snack. The mood under our tarp suddenly lightened.

We had a big, hot dinner and allowed the students to sleep in the next morning. We awoke to warm sunshine and nearly dried gear. Our students seemed to rebound well from this calamity. They were able to joke with each other about the dramatic events of the previous day.

> *"There is a certain unexplained comfort in temporary discomfort – the keyword being temporary."*

I often reflect on these forty-eight hours from the expedition as not only a watershed moment for all of us but also a pivotal moment for my entire life as an outdoor enthusiast. I have looked for and achieved challenges in my outdoor adventure pursuits. From swimming across the Chesapeake Bay several times to thru-hiking the Appalachian Trail, to doing a multi-pitch rock climbing ascent over nine hundred feet at Seneca Rocks, WV. But this particular expedition stands alone in reframing how I perceive challenge, adversity, risk, and resilience.

We take risks in so many aspects of our lives, often without a lot of forethought. We take calculated risks, whether we realize it or not, whenever we step outside our comfort zone. Risk-taking can be readily achieved in the wild, open spaces of the great outdoors or any new or novel space. The farther we go – first physically, then mentally, and finally emotionally – the more we evolve to become a collection of these experiences and a more refined version of our true selves. It starts with setting the table for success through education, training, preparing, and practicing for "what if." Embracing and promoting the impressive power of nature involves reshaping our heads and hearts. We need to stretch ourselves far enough to be present and mindful in that novel space, which we must make sense of and learn from. But not so far that we encounter sensory overload and either shut down or choose to never participate in that experience again. We cannot always predict how our outdoor adventures will play out. The more we push outside the lines of our comfort zone, the more we learn to trust – even that which we cannot control.

Having a previous experience to draw on from our time in the great outdoors (whether framed as a positive or a negative) builds a base layer of analytics in our brain which we can recall when in those environments again. One can even tap into these resources and use them in other relevant applications in one's life. There is a certain unexplained comfort in temporary discomfort – the keyword being temporary. That is why it is so important to understand the difference between controlled or perceived danger and true risks to our safety. This temporary discomfort may be justified because when we are on the other side, we can better appreciate the moment we were previously in. And from this experience, we can reflect, learn and ultimately, grow.

We as humans need to get out of this negative feedback loop of fight/flight/freeze mode and just take a step back and breathe and think. So why stretch? Why did George Mallory want to summit Mount Everest? "Because it was there," he said. We all have our own versions of Mount Everest that we see as challenges in our lives. If we don't stretch toward these challenges, we end up living a rather mundane life which can limit our opportunities – both personally and professionally.

Harnessing Distress Tolerance

We must embrace the ambiguous line between comfort and panic. Almost all progress in our lives takes place outside our comfort zone. And it is through adverse and challenging experiences we grow our comfort, stretch, and panic zones – and ultimately our resilience. The act of trying is an endeavor in optimism. If you are not somewhat uncomfortable, you are not really learning or growing to your potential.

Outside the Comfort Zone

- When is the last time you stepped out of your comfort zone?
- Describe how this made you feel.
- The basic idea of distress tolerance is to learn how to make it through a bad situation without making it worse. What helps you tolerate stress more effectively?
- When you find yourself outside the comfort zone, try to improve the moment. Which ideas are you open to trying?

Use of imagery

Deep breathing

Listening to music

Asking for help

Finding someone to talk to

Sending yourself compassion

Comfort, Stretch, and Panic

Reflect and write about instances in nature that created comfort, stretched you, and put you in the panic zone. What did you learn from those experiences?

Bryan Gomes

has almost two decades of environmental and outdoor education, water sports pursuits, public outreach, and team-building experience to his credit. He has an M.Ed. in Post-Secondary Education from Salisbury University. Bryan is enthusiastic about the outdoors and has thru-hiked the Appalachian Trail, from Georgia to Maine; kayaked the entire Chesapeake Bay from Havre de Grace, MD to the Atlantic Ocean, and as a lifeguard, lived in a tent on Assateague Island. Bryan embraces international travel and culture and has spent time in New Zealand, The Galapagos, and Cuba in recent years. Bryan is the Education Coordinator for ClearSharkH2O, an environmental education program to inspire a passion for waterways. He lives in Annapolis near the shores of the Severn River and enjoys paddling, fishing, cooking, beekeeping, and moonlights as a DJ.

Truth in the Saddle:

Learning to show up

I believe that horses bring out the best in us. They demand standards of behavior and levels of kindness that we, as humans, then strive to maintain.

~Clare Balding

"You're up! Start counting your strides. Get her going!" Ana yelled to me across the field. I barely squeezed my calves against her barrel, and Chessie quickened her pace from a trot to a canter. My mind began to race, "Keep your heels down, start counting her strides! She's going too fast!" We turned the corner to the jump, and her gait moved into a gallop. I was losing control. I pulled back on the reins in an attempt to slow her down, but she raced faster forward. I was new to horseback riding, newer to jumping, and barely acquainted with Chessie.

Ana continued yelling, "Slow her down! You are way too fast." I pulled harder on the reins, but she continued galloping. As we neared the small jump, I began to lose my balance on the saddle. A half-hour earlier, as I was preparing for my lesson, I had struggled to tighten her girth, the piece of equipment used to keep the saddle in place. Every time I pulled the strap around her barrel, she would turn her head and bite at me. Afraid to ask for help from the instructor and embarrassed to look unknowledgeable in front of my peers, I had left the girth loose before mounting. I had planned to tighten it later, but I never did.

I was barely hanging on to her mane and the reins as my right foot came out of the stirrup, and I began to lean to the left. At this point, my instructor's voice became background noise in the horror film that was projecting into my mind. I envisioned

Chessie stopping before the jump and my body flipping over her head. But Chessie had other plans. She cleared the jump with what felt like six feet to spare, and as soon as she landed, my body and the saddle slid to the left, and I quickly plummeted to the ground. To my surprise, I did not stop moving. My foot was caught in the stirrup iron and Chessie dragged me alongside her with no signs of slowing down. She continued running with me by her side down the field towards the woods. Just as we closed in on the wooded path, I wiggled my foot to freedom. Relief that I survived was quickly deflated by the embarrassment and shame that followed. I felt my face fill with hot humiliation. Ana yelled down the field to me, "Go get your horse!" My horse? Chessie was not my horse, nor did I want her to be. I was angry at her and did not want to ride her again.

Luckily, this event did not scare me away from horses. I wrote off the experience with Chessie as bad luck, an off day. I did not personalize it, and that helped me stay open to other equine experiences. I noticed that my body felt comfortable and relaxed when I was in the company of equines. This feeling inspired me to take workshops to become an equine-assisted psychotherapist. Equine Assisted Psychotherapy, often referred to as EAP, allows people to work on mental health issues, specific life goals, or personal growth with the assistance of horses.

Like most workshops, after a series of demonstrations and lectures, the facilitators ask participants to practice what they learned. I was assigned to a group of four humans including myself. Two people played the role of the facilitator team, and the other two played the clients. When it was my turn to play the role of the client, my partner and I were asked to create a scenario and act it out. He decided that we should be a married couple having communication issues. I went along with the role, but inside I was not comfortable with it. I was hoping to play a mother and child or two business partners, anything except a romantic relationship. At the time, I was having issues with a boyfriend, and the last thing I wanted to do during a work event was think about that. I kept my mouth closed and played along.

We introduced ourselves to the mock facilitators and told them our issues. They asked us to walk over and introduce ourselves to the horses. As I walked across the arena all I could think about was how angry I was about this lame activity. I approached one of the horses, and she moved away from me. I went over to the other horse. She walked away, too. I followed her and began to pet her mane, but she turned her head away. When we finished our visit and returned to the group, one mock facilitator asked if I noticed the horses turn away from me three times. I was angry that they would bring this up, so I came out of my role as a client and disclosed my true feelings about the exercise. I said, "You can never act around horses, they will always reflect your truth. They will sense that you are not being congruent." Time and time again, this statement has rung true.

I thought back to my ride with Chessie almost twenty years earlier. Not only was I terrified of jumping that day, but I was also afraid of messing up, doing it wrong, getting in trouble, and not being good enough. My thoughts were everywhere except in the present moment with her. Chessie cannot talk and tell us what she was feeling, but the energy those thoughts produced would make anyone want to run away. Horses have taught me to show up as I am. I have begun a practice of saying how I feel when I approach a horse to ensure that I am congruent. For example, I might say, "I am feeling fear right now, but I am coming to meet you anyway. Here I am, just as I am."

I continued my education in EAP through Natural Lifemanship–a trauma-informed, equine-assisted psychotherapy. This approach emphasizes that horses are more than a mirror and more than a metaphor, they are sentient beings, and–like humans–they thrive in healthy connected relationships. Horses are prey animals which means they have brains that prioritize survival and work hard to ensure safety at all times. Because of this, horses are keenly aware of their environment and constantly scan for potential danger. The part of the brain that is activated is called the brainstem and limbic system.

Humans, too, can often feel on edge and anxious and live from their "survival brains." Healthy connected relationships for both horses and humans help to create a sense of wellbeing. A connected partnership between the horse and the human can change both creatures at a neurological level. When horses and humans feel safe, they can activate a part of the brain called the neocortex. This part of the brain allows for play, trust, connection, and critical thinking. The tools that work for regulating the human brain and horse brain are similar. For example, when I experience anxiety or fear I have learned to soothe myself by moving in rhythmic ways. If I begin to sway, rock, or walk, my body will downshift, and I will induce a part of the nervous system called the parasympathetic nervous system that tells my brain to calm down. This is the same reason that rocking a baby helps soothe their crying. Horses, too, calm down when they experience rhythmic, patterned, repetitive movement.

"Healthy connected relationships for both horses and humans help to create a sense of wellbeing. A connected partnership between the horse and the human can change both creatures at a neurological level."

A few years ago, I worked with a dysregulated horse who was running in circles, bucking, and seemed very frightened. I stood a few yards away from him and began to swing a rope slowly and in a figure-eight shape. I continued to regulate my breathing and sway my body from side to side. Slowly, the horse calmed down and came to stillness. Once we both moved out of our survival brains, we communicated effectively with each other.

But how does one form a relationship with a horse? The principles are the same as those we use to create human relationships. Natural Lifemanship created the phrase and practice of Relationship Logic. It states horses can be active participants in this partnership, and they can make choices rather than simply submit to humans. If we desire a healthy connection with a horse, we must make requests and apply pressure. In human relationships, we do the same. For example, when you want to have lunch with a friend, you must apply pressure by asking your friend. She has three possible responses: she can say no to your request, she can ignore it, or she can say yes to it. Horses have the same options. The difference is that horses do not speak your dialect, but if you observe a horse herd or work with an equine specialist, you can learn their forms of communication and use it to practice connection with them.

Horses and humans feel safer in relationships. The practice of making requests, applying pressure, and forming healthy attachments with horses reorganizes the neurological connections in the brain and allows both the horse and the person to transform relationship patterns. Let us use my brief experience with Chessie as an example.

As a young teen, I was very afraid of making requests. I often did not want to ask for what I needed for fear that my needs were too much. Likewise, if someone did something I did not like, I was reluctant to confront it and instead would ask my mom or someone else to speak for me. Chessie had learned that if she nipped at people who put her saddle on, she would get them to stop. After years of having new riders on her back, she also learned to pull on the reins to protect her mouth.

Both our past relational patterns played out on that fateful day. If we had the time to get to know one another better, and had someone helping us see these patterns, we would have been able to develop a new relational dance. Horses have taught me how to speak up and be clear about my needs in human relationships. I can now honor myself and my needs by using clear communication.

Richard Louv, the author of Our Wild Calling, discusses the concept of mutual love in animal/human relationships. He states, "Whether animals are capable of love as we know it (though most of us believe they are), animals do bring us into contact with other people. They act as anti-rumination agents. They pull us out of ourselves and bring us into ourselves. They lead us home."

Twenty-three years ago, I was so focused on my appearance and how to properly ride a horse without looking stupid that I missed both, the animal in front of me and the true self within me. It was not until my only agenda was connection, that a horse led me home to learn more about my inner landscape and my capacity for love and relationship.

That relationship did not happen overnight. I had to practice congruence, boundaries, and leadership. As I continue to grow my relationships with equines, my human relationships also flourish. Today, when I experience conflict in my life, I often think, "How would this play out in the pasture?" These relationship principles are universal and I am grateful I learned them through my time with horses.

When Horses Teach Us

My experience with Equine-Assisted Psychotherapy has transformed my perception of horses. I always knew they were special and offered me peace, but I never knew how or why. The examples in this chapter demonstrate that horses are highly sensitive beings and always live in the present moment. When I join them in those moments, I, too, become present and mindful of my thoughts and behaviors.

Practical ways to foster self-awareness around a horse

- **Relational Observation:** Mindfully observe horses in a herd with all five of your senses. Notice how they interact. Allow yourself to see how horses apply pressure on one another? How do they do this? What is their non-verbal body language? Do you notice a leader of the group? What behaviors tell you that they are the leader? What behaviors tell you they are not a leader in the herd? Do you relate to any of the horses? Which ones? Why?

- **Notice your Body:** The next time you are with a horse, notice the sensations in your body. What happens? Where do you feel this? Can you put a label on what you are feeling? Does the feeling change or shift in relation to the horse's actions? Notice if your mind makes up a story about these sensations. Can you let the story go and come back only to the feelings?

- **Get Congruent:** Clinical professor of psychiatry and best-selling author Daniel Siegel has coined the phrase, "Name it to tame it." He is referring to identifying our emotions. If we can name the feeling, we validate it and have a better chance of integrating it. The next time you are in an uncomfortable, vulnerable, or even joyful experience, before trying to hide or cover up your true feelings, label the emotion in your mind or aloud. Next, honor that you feel this way. If you are in the presence of a horse when you do this, even better.

- Bottom-Up Regulation: Rhythmic patterned repetitive movement calms both the horse and the human brain. It regulates the lower parts of the brain called the brainstem and diencephalon. When these areas are calmer, we can access the power of the higher portion of the brain called the neocortex. From this place, we can think through a challenge.
  - **Practice without a horse.** Regulating your lower brain is very helpful in a stressful situation, but why wait for an emergency? Stand up and begin moving by slowly marching in place. Notice the back and forth movement of your body as you pick up one foot and then the other. Now begin to clap your hands and sway with the rhythm of your feet. Do this for at least two minutes. Afterwards, you may notice feeling more in balance or lighter. If you like, add music that has a rhythm you enjoy. Allow yourself to be immersed and soothed by the movement.
  - **Practice with horses.** If you are in a situation that brings up fear or tension when you are with a horse, first regulate yourself. Move your feet back and forth, sway your body, or clap your hands softly and rhythmically. Next, begin to regulate your breathing. Breathe into your belly and slowly release through an extended exhale. If the horse appears dysregulated, your rhythmic, patterned repetitive movement can also help him. You may begin swinging a lead rope in a figure-eight or a circular pattern. This input will begin to calm the horse. Give it time.

Tracy Sanna

received her Master of Science in Clinical Counseling with a focus on spiritually integrated psychotherapy from Loyola University Maryland. She began her career as a therapist at two different acute care facilities, helping teens and adults work through issues including substance abuse, self-harm, depression, anxiety, and PTSD. Since then, she has worked as an out-patient private practice therapist in Maryland. In addition to counseling, she finds joy in teaching. She taught middle school and high school for ten years and is currently teaching undergraduate Psychology. Tracy moved to San Diego from Baltimore, Maryland at the beginning of 2022 and is deeply enjoying the beauty of the west coast.

III.

NATURE AS COUNSELOR

From Sorrow to Solace

PREFACE:
The emotional benefit of being attached to nature

Covid-19 is currently wreaking havoc in most corners of the world. The practice of social distancing and the use of face coverings remind us daily that a real threat is amongst us. As we strive to keep ourselves and others safe, our mental health is suffering. With anxiety and depression on the rise and grief a communal experience, a common place of solace has emerged: the outdoors. Camping gear is sold out. Kayak rentals have a waiting list. Hiking trails are busier than the mall. People are flocking outside as if a cure awaits at the trailhead. And perhaps it does.

So, what is this siren call of the woods and ocean? John Muir experienced this himself. He speaks about the wind's power to remove our cares.

Who doesn't need some cares to drop off like leaves? From Muir's standpoint, the value of exploring humankind's connection with the natural world is essential to the health of individuals, societies, and the planet as a whole. In my academic research, I've read numerous studies that established that connection to nature was associated with positive emotions, vitality, autonomy, personal growth, and purpose in life.

There seems to be an innate need, a hardwiring of some sort, that drives us outdoors, that has over six million people tune in as David Attenborough's Planet Earth brings nature onto our TV screens. Once we follow that inner urging and feel the forest floor or the sand under our feet, a deep exhale escapes our tense bodies, and our overtaxed nervous system begins to unwind. The sound of water, birdsong, or gentle wind embraces us and whispers of long-forgotten times when nature was our dwelling place.

At the Center for Nature Informed Therapy, we walk alongside people who need improved mental wellness. People crippled with anxiety, dead with depression, or destroyed by a loss can experience pain that seems daunting, yet it never ceases to amaze me how "natural" it is to introduce nature as my co-therapist. This is the type of therapist you can rely on and who will be there throughout your life in the form of mountains, trees, flowers, oceans, birds, and butterflies. Nature's credentials are ancient and unembellished, promising to guide you from a place of sorrow to a place of solace.

"Being in nature is not only inspiring, but it also has medical and psychotherapeutic potential. By experiencing nature, we place our body in the original functional circle made of humans and the environment from which we emerged. We put two matching puzzle pieces together – us and nature into one whole."

~Clemens G. Arvay

ON EDGE WITH ANXIETY:
A green heron leads the way out

"I had also started to recognize just how positive I felt when I was immersed in the world of birds. My worries seemed to fade into insignificance and when I was feeling stressed, if I counteracted it with some time outside, watching them, it drifted off like birds do, in a stiff breeze."

~Joe Harkness

It defied logic. I was young(ish) and physically healthy, married to a wonderful person, had a job that I genuinely enjoyed, owned a starter house in a beautifully wooded neighborhood, and was the father of two adorable, clever, little boys. My life was good, really good. But internally, I was experiencing extreme anxiety. By my fortieth birthday, I was no longer able to suppress what was a part of my very fiber—an inability to prioritize. I kept making small issues—minor annoyances, for most people—take on enormous importance in my mind.

As is so often the case, financial angst was the original impetus of my journey down a long path of overblown fears and out-of-proportion worrying. By the time our second son arrived, our little duplex had become uncomfortably tight for a family of four. We searched for a roomier, yet affordable house—unfortunately, right as the unprecedented housing bubble of the 2000s neared its peak. After moving too slowly and being outbid on several occasions, we decided on a gamble. Before we had put our original house on the market, we made an offer that was at the top of our budgeted price range and barely within my comfort zone. The offer was accepted, a closing date set, and we had two months to sell one home before taking ownership of a second. Those two months remain a complete blur in my mind; clearly, the risk had been too much for me. I went into hyperdrive, working around the clock to repair, clean, and tackle every task conceivable to make our humble home attractive to would-be buyers and avoid the impending disaster if we did not sell promptly.

In the end, the financial ruin I had envisioned never came. A quote often attributed to Mark Twain befits this anxious time in my life, "I have known a great many troubles, but most of them never happened." Nonetheless, in just two months of utter panic, I had developed some terrible habits: endless worrying, giving credence to thoughts as if they were real, and ignoring my body's need for rest. With each successive stressor, they gradually worsened. Minor disagreements with supervisors at work, fairly typical, middle-aged health problems—over the next few years with each such setback, I assumed the worst possible outcome, and my propensity to worry ramped up another notch. It took several years of therapy and a very intentional reconnection with a pastime from my youth to calm my constant anxieties.

In hindsight, what most surprises me is not that I entered this bleak, fearful period in my life, but that I had been able to avoid it for so long. Admittedly, for the most part, my childhood was relatively carefree. We had a close-knit family and lived a modest, middle-class existence in small-town Pennsylvania. I played youth sports, took music lessons, and, weather permitting, was usually outdoors, playing ball of some sort with neighborhood friends. Still, my childhood was not without challenges, as I grew up with a mother who battled her entire life with obsessive-compulsive disorder. Only a few of my closest buddies ever figured out why they were rarely invited inside our house; issues surrounding cleanliness were the most difficult for mom. She routinely became annoyed over a bit of mud on the floor or a minor spill in the kitchen. A kid with a runny nose or mild cough entering her home was too much for her to handle. My father, my sister, and I gradually learned to tiptoe around mom's pet peeves. The entire daily schedule often had to be adjusted to fit around her need to finish some major cleaning project or to check off a few more 'to do' tasks. As I grew older, however, I became increasingly aware of—and saddened by—how often my mom was on edge and how rarely she seemed relaxed.

Interestingly, one of the few times my mother seemed able to decompress and become truly present in the moment was when we were out in nature looking for birds. It was not always easy to convince mom to let herself go birding, but once she was outdoors, the sights, smells, and sounds of nature won her over immediately. A leisurely walk in the fresh air did wonders for her mood, and the open-endedness of the task at hand—find, observe, and enjoy these colorful, melodic wonders of nature—made hours melt away, often without even a glance at her watch.

Anxious people, especially those with obsessive tendencies, are at their worst when they are not busy. An idle mind is their greatest enemy, as they beat themselves up thinking of all the things which could happen, instead of appreciating things that are happening. When engaged with nature, there are so many things to observe and discover that it becomes virtually impossible to participate with anxious thoughts. As the noise of everyday life becomes replaced with the songs of birds, one is forced to let go of future concerns and instead becoming intensely focused on the present.

Perhaps what I appreciated most about my mother's approach to birding was her ability to find wonderment, even within the ordinary and common. At its most extreme, the hobby can lead to unhealthy compulsions. A small but growing number of enthusiasts are driven by a constant need to add to 'the list.' They drop everything

and hop in the car to pick up a 'lifer' two states away or fly off to exotic lands whenever their budget allows, in search of novelties to jack up their species count, a bragging right for some.

> *"When engaged with nature, there are so many things to observe and discover that it becomes virtually impossible to participate with anxious thoughts. As the noise of everyday life becomes replaced with the songs of birds, one is forced to let go of future concerns and instead becoming intensely focused on the present."*

Sure, our family sometimes planned vacations around new birding opportunities, but mom, in particular, never lost appreciation for the familiar birds she encountered every day. Her favorite sound was the soulful cooing of the ubiquitous mourning dove. She was the only family member persistent enough to coax our resident chickadees to hand-feed. Even non-birding friends were impressed when mom trained the local pair of mockingbirds to come in response to her whistle whenever she refilled their bowl of currants. Had she ever made one, mom's birding highlight reel would have consisted almost entirely of sentimental favorites, not one-hit wonders.

Truly one of my most memorable birding experiences took place just a few miles from home. I was hiking alone and happened upon a small green heron hunting just feet from the shoreline of a local reservoir. My timing was perfect, as I became privy to the entire sequence of it stalking, spearing, and eventually swallowing a massive bullfrog. I was entranced by the protracted predator-prey struggle and became completely lost in the moment, unaware that thirty-five minutes had passed, and I had not moved. A special nature moment like that is a gift—almost ethereal in

its ability to capture my undivided attention, remove me from whatever pesky thoughts were cluttering my mind, and leave me in absolute awe of the natural world and the intricate relationships among its creatures.

I don't know how well I would be functioning today if I had not found birding as a kid. Originally, I tried to keep my hobby a secret from peers. I was outed in a most public way when, in the middle of ninth-grade history class, a uniquely quizzical announcement came booming over the P.A. system, "Brian Rollfinke, please come to the office. Your parents are here to take you to see…an owl?!?" Following the long pause, one could hear complete bewilderment in the tone of those last two words. Turns out that a snowy owl, one of birding's most desired grail birds, was sunning in a farm field just two miles from school. A 'lifer' for all of us, the opportunity was too good to pass up, and my folks decided to pull me from class to go see it. Naturally, I took some good-hearted ribbing from friends for a long time. By college, however, my self-consciousness faded, and birding became a significant part of my identity. It remained so until the all-consuming responsibilities of full-time employment, homeownership, and starting a family left my binoculars collecting dust for the better part of two decades.

It was a tragic loss that led me to reconnect with nature. In 2011, we lost my only sibling, my little sister, at the extremely premature age of forty-one, to a pulmonary embolism. In the years prior, she had struggled mightily with OCD and depression; unlike Mom and me, she had never been bitten by the birding bug. Several months later and rather out of the blue, mom suggested a family trip as a healing step in the grieving process. We chose Arizona for its uniqueness relative to other regions of the country with which we were better acquainted. Also, we suspected our sons, then ages thirteen and nine, would enjoy encountering an entirely new

array of wildlife. This proved to be an immense understatement. None of us anticipated the sheer excitement that the fauna of the Southwest ignited in those boys. Sure, they were understandably thrilled to see black bears, coyotes, and pronghorns; but they were equally fascinated by roadrunners, quail, and the colorful variety of hummingbirds. Almost overnight, the very youngsters whose needs had necessitated my putting birding on the back shelf were now clamoring for us to venture out into nature at every opportunity. Those three weeks marked a real turning point for my emotional well-being but, more importantly, also kindled in my children a genuine interest in hiking, photography, and nature.

We still head outdoors together frequently. The shared experience always brings us closer. As the Arizona trip did for me, immersion in nature has helped all of us cope with subsequent losses and sorrow; sadly, beginning with my mom's death in 2018, the boys have lost three grandparents in as many years. Throughout this challenging period for our family, ventures into the outdoors, both together and alone, have allowed each of us time for meaningful introspection and space to process our grief.

I have found that when walking in nature, my recollections of joyful memories from the past are more vivid and my ability to find hope among despair is enhanced. Not surprisingly, it is while birding, that I sometimes converse with my deceased mother which in turn brings me peace and gives me a sense of balance. Isn't this precisely the goal for anyone trying to overcome an anxiety disorder and regain their sense of equilibrium? Take away balance/stability and flight becomes freefall. Thankfully, for three generations in my family, we have found ourselves far more able to soar on the wings of birds.

The Birds are Awaiting

Start simple. All you need is a modest pair of binoculars and a field guide. If you're able, set up a few feeders or birdhouses in your yard and become familiar with the handful of species that frequent them. The better you know those, the more readily you will detect when someone less common appears. Once you start heading out farther afield, you will want comfortable walking shoes and bland outerwear that does not boldly announce your presence; leave the bubblegum pink jacket at home.

Make time. Trying to cram a quick birding outing into a hectic schedule rarely works. Birding is at its most enjoyable and especially beneficial when it is relatively unstructured, without rigid time restrictions.

Go big. Early on, focus on larger species, like waterfowl or raptors, as it is easier to observe their field marks. You'll have plenty of time to learn about the little brown birds later.

Save fossil fuels. No need to continually venture into new territory. There is much to be said for having a few favorite local parks or public spaces, visiting them often, and knowing them well. Regular visits can lead to insight into the seasonal timing of the plant community and the organisms that depend on it.

Make it a family affair. Solo birding has its benefits, but the hobby can be highly social, too. Who better to accompany you on long walks in the woods than family members or close friends? Furthermore, from a spotting perspective, an extra set of eyes and ears can always help in the field. And do not worry that your kids are too young. I started birding at the age of ten.

Tech is okay; just no calls. While one of the greatest benefits of birding is the large blocks of unplugged time, cell phones are not a complete no-no. There is a wealth of technological resources designed to help new birders learn. Websites such as eBird and iNaturalist and free apps like Merlin can demystify identifications, explain behaviors and abundance patterns, and help locate the best nearby places to find target species.

Join the flock. Seek out local birding clubs online and attend some of their educational programs. Birders, on the whole, are a warm and welcoming bunch; they generally have a lot to share and always include several cute slides in their presentations.

Don't be hard on yourself. Everyone (yes, everyone) makes misidentifications from time to time. Just better to run things by a local expert, if you are unsure, before posting a finding online that will bring out 'twitchers' the next morning.

Contribute data. As your skills improve, build some regularity into your birding schedule by engaging in long-term citizen science projects, like Cornell's Project FeederWatch or statewide Breeding Bird Atlases. You will benefit from more sustained stress relief and feel good about adding purpose to your outings. Before long, you will find yourself looking forward to these occasions of being an amateur ornithologist.

Pay it forward. When the opportunity arises for a small act of kindness, share your knowledge with others. On numerous occasions, I have stopped non-birding passers-by to show them an active nest, an unusually close raptor, or a real stunner, a male Baltimore oriole, for instance. It invariably embarrasses my sons but is always appreciated by those with whom I share.

Brian Rollfinke

became interested in birds as a child, thanks to a local college professor, who invited him to observe, then eventually help, for several seasons at a small bird-banding operation in the mountains of Central Pennsylvania. Brian went on to earn a B.S. in Biology from Wake Forest University, then an M.S. in Ecology, with a focus on forest songbirds, from Penn State. His career in environmental science was put on hold for a brief thirty-one years, during which he taught math and coached baseball at a Baltimore independent school, got married, and raised two sons, who share his passion for orioles (both those found in sycamores and the dugout.) Various citizen science projects occupied whatever free time Brian had during those busy decades. After finally deciding what he wanted to be when he grew up, Brian signed on as Director of Education at Irvine Nature Center, outside Baltimore, in January of 2020. He couldn't be happier.

A Blade of Grass:
Freedom from addiction in the web of life

Out beyond ideas of wrongdoing and rightdoing,
There is a field, I'll meet you there.
When the soul lies down in that grass,
The world is too full to talk about.
Ideas, language, even the phrase 'each other'
Doesn't make any sense.
~Rumi

When I was a child, the inside of my home felt tense, scary, and ill-fitting, so I would go outside. Riding my bike, climbing trees, and sneaking through a local tree farm restored my feelings of independence, confidence, and joy. I believed that inside my home I had no power, but outside I was mighty.

At school, I was constantly being asked to sit down, stop talking, stop reading during lessons, stop doodling, sit still and listen; I felt like there was something wrong with me because I just could not do it. Sitting still, being quiet, and listening felt like punishments. Teachers' conferences and medication became routine, and it established an idea of myself that something was wrong with me. But during recess and those blissful summer vacations, that was not the case. I could run through the woods like a deer, climbed trees higher than any of my friends would dare, and achieved a belief in myself. I was a powerful witch making muddy potions in the wells created by tree roots and healing the world through my communications with the realm of the forest spirits. Inside, nobody wanted to hear me; outside, my voice reached the sky.

When I got my driver's license and a car, I began skipping school regularly. I would almost always end up at a local reservoir. By this time my drinking and drug use had begun, and I maintained my association of being outside with being the best and happiest version of myself. But, as John Stewart's character in the movie Half Baked would ask, "Have you ever tried being the best and happiest version of yourself, on weed?" Well, I did, with the additional experiments of alcohol and drugs, and it was great for a long time. When I was outside, drunk and high, nothing could touch me: not fear, not insecurity, not dread, nothing. I had spent a short lifetime pushing down feelings and already my inner reservoir was full and my dam failing. Retreating outside was not effective on its own anymore, my self-loathing and insecurity found me where I once felt so safe; but with drugs and alcohol as allies, I could temporarily get back to that place of peace, power, and confidence.

In recovery programs, we are asked to "look back, but don't stare". Reflecting on my early years, I realize I was getting messages from the human world which did not carry a high level of esteem. School, grades, and status, I was told, were important while being strong, curious, and free seemed threatening to success. I went back to nature again and again. Nature became my sanctuary for ways to cope with the "real world." Mother Nature whispered in my ear that I was just right, while the adults and other children around me bellowed through megaphones that I was not enough.

At a house out in the country one summer night during high school, my friends and I were drunk and on MDMA, a party drug that makes the user feel euphoric. I laid down on the lawn and looked up at the night sky. It was filled with stars. As I rested there, it occurred to me that the grass had no other recourse or expectation in its life than to do exactly what I was doing at that moment. I was overcome with wonder and envy and remember being exhilarated with the epiphany. I called my friends over and begged them to lie down near me and just be a blade of grass. I don't know what their experience was, but we laughed and breathed, and just laid there for a long time until, one by one, we abandoned the experiment and rejoined the party. I have asked many groups of people to be blades of grass since that night. To this day, I relish the opportunity to abandon the burden of consciousness, stop holding on to the past, ignore a looming future, and forget feelings of hurt, fear, and loss. By becoming a blade of grass, I feel like I am perhaps performing my highest calling: "beingness" a term I learned from Mooj, a Jamaican spiritual teacher.

"Nature became my sanctuary for ways to cope with the 'real world.' Mother Nature whispered in my ear that I was just right."

I believe that my addiction to drugs and alcohol stemmed from the desire to feel connected. The message from what philosopher David Abrams calls the "more-than-human-world" let me believe that I am enough, powerful, and part of everything. While I wanted it more than anything to be true, I seemingly could only get to this state with the help of drugs. And they pulled me into a quagmire.

Deeply unhappy and sick, I ended up in a dangerous relationship with someone who was an alcoholic just like me. We got into a fight, and I went outside into the cold spring night and laid down on the lawn. I looked up at the stars and begged them to kill me. The euphoria of my early drinking and drug use had progressively led to devastation. Here among the blades of grass, I realized I needed to change.

When I began my journey in sobriety, I again turned to nature as a resource for my healing. I began by planting a large vegetable garden, which gave me a connection with the Earth, a daily discipline, and things that depended on me showing up. Then I started to learn about foraging, and my confidence soared as I met one edible or medicinal plant after another and was nourished, accepted, and healed by them. I found rewarding work in organizations with the mission of connecting people to nature. Through facilitating children's and adults' relationships with the natural world, mine renewed and grew. I have not stopped doing those things, and I am still sober today.

In nature, I have learned about the fortitude and patience of a tree, the persistence of water, the perfect use of energy in a bird's flight, and the interdependence of all. It finally occurred to me that by just being me, breathing, and existing, I connect to everything. My fears and insecurities fade away when the web of life holds me. I am an alcoholic with a progressive, incurable illness that is centered around my thinking, and I know that spending time outside has saved my life.

Be a Blade of Grass

This visually oriented meditation is best done outside, on a lawn, or in a meadow. You may enjoy laying on a blanket or towel.

1. Take off your shoes and lay down on your back.

2. Run your hands and feet across the grass for a few moments.

3. Consider the grass' existence: its start as a seed, its steady growth upwards, the rain, the hot sun, the chilly fall, the snow, the mud after the snow melts. All the while, the grass keeps living, slowly growing, minimally changed by the weather. Imagine the grass smiling maybe, loving every second of its life. Think about what the grass does all day and night.

4. Move your head from side to side, eye-level with the grass, and look at what it looks at.

5. Then turn your gaze upwards and spend a long time looking up at the sky. This is what the grass moves towards.

6. Imagine you are a blade of grass. Let go of your past, let go of your body, let go of your thoughts, and just be effortlessly alive, rooted in the earth, growing towards the sky.

Personal Reflections

- As the grass stretches toward the sky, it seems drawn upward by an unseen motivational force. What do you move towards? What makes up your motivational force?
- To be effortlessly alive, we are asked to let go. What past events do you need to let go of? What have you not forgiven yourself for?
- What negative judgments about your body do not serve you any longer?
- Make a list of recurring unhelpful stories or thoughts that need to be released.
- Rootedness suggests a found sense of stability within ourselves. A sense of our inherent goodness and safety. In your life, what creates that sense of rootedness?

Erin Quinley

is an outdoor educator with many years of personal and professional experience in leading groups of people in challenges and experiences in nature. She is a Wilderness First Responder, Leave No Trace trainer, Maryland Master Naturalist intern, and ropes course manager. She is passionate about connecting people to their inner wildness and nature.

Nature's Mothering:

Walking together on a road called grief

Sorrow is part of the Earth's great cycles, flowing into the night like cool air sinking down a river course. To feel sorrow is to float on the pulse of the Earth, the surge from living to dying, from coming into being to ceasing to exist. Maybe this is why the Earth has the power over time to wash sorrow into a deeper pool, cold and shadowed. And maybe this is why, even though sorrow never disappears, it can make a deeper connection to the currents of life and so connect, somehow, to sources of wonder and solace.

~Kathleen Dean Moore

On a cool September morning, my dad woke me and my sister up from our campsite on the couch to tell us that our mom had died. It was a Tuesday, I was freshly seventeen, and my mom had been sick—very sick—for a long time. I knew that she could die in the way that I knew that there are seven billion people in the world or that there are four hundred billion stars in our galaxy. It was a colossal truth my thinking mind could not begin to comprehend, so I kept it tucked safely in the dark waters of my subconscious, never really expecting to feel its full force.

In the years before her death, my mom and I would paint the tulips at the local botanical gardens as they reemerged, surprised every time how they remembered to bud and bloom. We would pick a quiet spot next to a grove of Japanese maples or by the duck pond and let our drug store paint brushes dance over the page, delighted by the fecundity around us. We were both amateur artists at best, but our subject's beauty more than made up for what we lacked in skill. I remember thinking how beautiful my mom looked in those moments; her blonde hair uncharacteristically pinned back and out of her professional wear that seemed to signify her stress. She laughed easily in the garden and her ease made me feel safe; all was right with the world.

As my mom's illness progressed, however, so did my adolescence. No amount of love between us could stop the inevitable butting of heads that must happen between mother and daughter. Chemotherapy had taken her golden hair and my sense of safety but rather than come closer to one another, our fear often pushed us further apart. Fights over the normal coming of age tensions were laden with deeper implications and our mounting dread of an inevitable separation caused endless misunderstandings. While in my heart of hearts, I longed to be close to her, in reality, I didn't want to be anywhere near her. The summer before she died, I jumped at the chance to go on a backwoods backpacking trip for two weeks with my friend's youth group. I was desperate to get out of my house, which felt heavy amidst bottles of pills and get-well cards.

During those two weeks in the woods, I came alive. I slept under tarps and the sky, and eventually even ceased to be horrified by my smell after fourteen days without a shower. Everything felt simple in the woods, and I loved how quickly life became about tending to your next, immediate need. Amidst the rivers and the trees, I felt myself connect with my own wildness and enjoyed the miracle of what my body could do. I set aside existential questions and enjoyed the satisfaction of a granola bar after a long stretch of hiking or laughing around the fire with my new tribe. I felt free.

My body was strong and tan by the time I returned home, which only further accentuated the gulf between my mom and me. It was as if while I was soaking up the sun and vitality, the last of hers was slipping away. I arrived home to find her in the hospital a frail shadow of herself. I longed to curl up with her in the hospital bed, lay my head on her shoulder, and have her tell me it would all be okay, but I feared my wish would break her. Gone was the freedom and joy of the woods and in its place was a fear of what felt like the ultimate goodbye. She died three weeks later.

One year later, during my freshman year of college, the pain of my grief had caught up with me in form of major depression. With my whole world in shambles, the wildness of the woods no longer felt like something I could trust, and instead, I opted for control and rigidity. I tried to be good, good, good in what I ate, what I thought, what I said, the grades I got, the clothes I wore, the thank-you notes I wrote, the prayers I prayed–all in a desperate attempt to restore some sense of order to the world around me. I saw my grief and sadness as something to exercise, expel, root out, and remove, rather than something to simply feel and tend to.

I still remember, with visceral detail, the first night I stepped away. I was in my dorm room with the walls closing in and all of a sudden, like a wild caged animal, I needed to GET OUT. I needed to go somewhere, anywhere, away from being inside. At the time, I thought it was my own skin I needed to escape, the need was primal and literal; I needed to be back somewhere that made sense, somewhere that did not feel so alien and suffocating. I needed to be outside.

Wordlessly, I left my boyfriend and my roommate behind, walked into the hallway, felt the weight of the cool aluminum door under my hands, and sprinted out

into the darkness. Instantly, I could feel my breath return. Then, I simply started to run. When I couldn't run any further, I walked. And I kept walking. There was something about the rhythmic motion of moving my feet under that black and blue night sky that settled me in a way I had not experienced before. Nothing made sense to me during the day. Daytime meant going to class and attempting to care about papers and punctuation, remembering to laugh at things people said, and trying to look like you were eating full meals. People talk about depression as apathy but don't be confused, no one will work harder on the outside than someone who feels dead on the inside. My daytimes were filled with the combination of toxic indifference and desperate longing all at once, masked by the anxious attempt to appear okay.

"People talk about depression as apathy but don't be confused, no one will work harder on the outside than someone who feels dead on the inside."

At night though, I just walked. I walked when the air was crisp and when it was heavy with humidity. I walked in light mist and heavy rain. I walked through well-manicured gardens and open park fields. I walked through shady oak groves and along quiet streams. The night soothed me. There was no judgment there. No way I was supposed to feel or nothing I was supposed to do or say or think. The night did not need anything from me, yet I took comfort in the fact that She was bigger than me and could hold me in a way I secretly was not even sure that God could. During the daytime, I was slowly being driven mad by an outsized sense of my importance and responsibility. But on my nighttime walks, I found a reprieve from feeling like I needed to make the sun rise and set. Mother Nature was on it.

"If there is one thing I have come to know about grief, it is that it is never predictable and anything but linear."

Throughout the intervening roughly two decades, it has been nature that has anchored me. If there is one thing I have come to know about grief, it is that it is never predictable and anything but linear. Healing from and living with depression has been the same. The tides of happiness and sadness ebb and flow. What nature has taught me, however, is that this is the way of things. She has taught me that the sun rises and it sets, that the leaves fall and return, that people, dreams, relationships, and identities die. And that it is all–dare I say–natural.

Ironically, something about the cool, detached void of the endless night sky was the comfort I needed to help me see that none of this needs to be judged and that no one even needs to answer for it. The biggest lesson nature continues to teach me is that somewhere, somehow, under all of the loss, there will always be a return. That what is gone from sight has only merely transformed for a while. That there is a deeper intelligence that reminds the buds when to bloom.

Nature mothered me when the pat answers of my youth no longer satisfied me. Even as I racked up degrees in theology, philosophy, and pastoral counseling, I had a sinking feeling that the whole set-up of heaven and hell, of good and evil, of sin and salvation, was not working for me anymore. Instead, I began to find heaven in the wildflowers and the way the light hit the first good snow of the year. My body, too, took solace in shifting from something to be perfected and purified to part of this glorious, messy whole. These days, "good" is a word I use to describe the way fresh raspberries taste in my mouth or the way my body feels when I walk barefoot for the first time in summer, rather than a perpetual state of morality or respectability to which I was aspiring.

It is even better when glimpses of heaven are in your backyard rather than a lifetime away when there is someone there you would like to talk to. Mother Nature has become my telephone line to my mom. Inevitably, driving or walking on a sunny day–often through the open countryside–the light will catch, and I will know she is right here with me, invisible to my eyes but not to my heart. She grew up by the sea, and I can always meet her there, too, in a piece of sea glass or driftwood or in the way the sky turns orange and pink when the sun is about to set. "The perfect time to eat mint chocolate chip ice cream," she would say. The Irish poet John O'Donohone speaks of the "thin places" where the veil between this world and the next is light and malleable. I have come to find that for me, these thin places can be accessed best anywhere where birds drown out cars, where stars outshine city lights, and where my feet can feel mud or sand beneath them.

Just recently, I returned to the woods. On my first night under the stars, I felt that same relief I did the night I rushed out of my dorm room; except this time, I was not running. My body was once again strong and tan and in touch with wildness and yet, fully aware of its fragility and mortality. The fact that my body will one day fade and die makes its vitality so precious and the chance to feel all of it so very sweet.

An Exploration of Eco-Grief

Many of us feel love, acceptance, and protection in our relationship with Mother Nature. Consequently, it has been hard to ignore the fact that she, like my mom, is sick, her cancer is our way of living that puts us at odds with her elegant wisdom. Every time we go a winter without snow or the humidity lasts far, far into the fall, I wince a little, longing to put my head on her shoulder and whisper to her that I know this is hard for her, "Shhhh, Mama rest, get some sleep!"

This time though, the grief I feel at watching parts of her fade does not stir up depression but rather a way of being more awake to her beauty. I want her to be well. I want her streams to be clear and her air to be pure. I want the majesty of her forests to be respected and all of her inhabitants to enjoy her abundance. Despite all the environmental destruction, I know that she will go on. She may disappear for a time, but only to reemerge as something new and (however could it be possible) more beautiful. And when she does, some part of me will be with her. And we will paint tulips together.

As someone who studies death, thanatologist Kriss Kevorkian defines environmental grief as "the grief reaction stemming from the environmental loss of ecosystems by natural and man-made events."

How aware are you of the "ecogrief" you experience on a day-to-day or season-to-season basis?

Are you taking time to grieve nature the way you would grieve a loved one? If so, are you allowing your grief to propel you into deeper appreciation and action, or are you being pulled under into a current of despair?

Alongside your practice of lament, consider focusing on what you can control. Action can inspire a sense of hope. Select an area of eco-activism that feels personally meaningful. For example, if you have an affinity for trees, consider supporting the Old-Growth Forest Network and help them champion native forests.

(www.oldgrowthforest.net)

Finally, don't underestimate the power of community. Many others experience deep pain around the loss of habitats and inaction to climate solutions. Check out groups such as the Good Grief Network.

(www.goodgriefnetwork.org).

Kate Gerwin

is a licensed professional counselor and certified nature-informed counselor. Kate graduated from Loyola University Maryland in a program with a spiritually integrated emphasis and has worked in a variety of clinical mental health settings, as a teacher, and as a school counselor. Kate has completed numerous trainings in mindfulness, breathwork, and nutrition and has a passion for addressing the whole person mind, body, and spirit.

Hunting for Peace:
A mountain helps with traumatic stress

I do not hunt for the joy of killing but for the joy of living, and the inexpressible pleasure of mingling my life however briefly, with that of a wild creature that I respect, admire and value.

– John Madson

If I think about them, the memories come back quickly, raw. First the pause. Then the realization that something traumatic was going to happen. Next a loud crunch, then quiet, then the sound of glass exploding, then quiet. Finally a crash. I have always wondered what people meant when they said things slowed down in a moment of crisis, but now I know distinctly.

My truck was on its side in the ditch beyond the shoulder. Gravity was pulling me upside down. I unbuckled my seatbelt and fell to the partially crushed cab of the truck. I crawled out the broken window and then realized the engine was still running. I climbed back through the window and turned the key in the ignition. It was over. I was alive.

Leading up to the accident, I had spent a week twenty-five miles from the nearest pavement hiking up steep inclines among pine trees, Oregon grape, Kinnickinnic, and bunchgrass. I had drawn a coveted bighorn sheep ram tag, and this was the first week of a hunting season that lasted a month and a half. The rain started the first day and did not stop the entire week. I had good gear and a teepee with a stove to dry off at night, so I was fairly comfortable.

This first trip was about getting the lay of the land and testing my fitness. I found a band of ewes and some young rams. The rain wore on me, but I got in some good reading with "The Dog Stars" by Peter Heller. The story takes place in post-apocalyptic times with the main character finding solace in some of the remaining flora and fauna that surround him. Without giving away the ending, there was a reunion at the close that made me pine for my wife.

The constant rain, the steep hills, the loneliness. I just needed to go home and rekindle the fire. Following days of unrelenting rain, everything I had brought with me was soaked. Instead of packing away all my gear, I stuffed it in the backseat of my truck. Suddenly, my desire to leave was so strong that I broke camp quickly, then headed down the long, bumpy dirt road toward home. The ride was enjoyable although it smelled like four wet Labrador retrievers were riding with me. My spirits were high. I was heading home and had garnered some good information for the remainder of my hunt.

When I finally hit the pavement, the first place I could get cell service, I anxiously phoned my wife. No answer. That was okay, as I was now only a half-hour from home, on good roads, and my favorite fried chicken was at the next exit. As I pulled off, my mind returned to my wife, and I attempted to call her once more. Why I decided not to wait just one more minute will forever be a question I ask myself. It was dark and the light of the phone sucked me in. I drifted to the left on the soft shoulder, soaked by a week of rain. I hit a small reflector post, overcorrected, lost control, and found myself headed for a large highway sign anchored by two steel posts. The sheer explosion of force was impressive and scary. I had to be grateful to be alive.

When I finally made it home that night, I was shaken. I had cut my hands when I crawled back into the truck and my shoulders hurt, the left one in particular. Besides that, physically I was unscathed. I hugged my wife and kids tighter and longer than usual and then tried to get some rest. I was exhausted. Sleep did not come that night, nor for the next few nights. The sounds of the crash kept playing in my mind every time I closed my eyes. I do not know if it was the pain in my shoulders, but I could not get comfortable, tossing and turning, keeping my bedmate up. I felt the urge to find a dark hole and just crawl in it. The thought of driving again was chilling.

And yet, I had the tug and the pressure of a once-in-a-lifetime hunt for a coveted bighorn ram, and the clock was ticking. Should I stay home where it was safe and heal my body and spirit? Or should I push past the barrier and head back to the mountain?

I needed to head back. I was disrupting my wife's sleep, and could not find rest myself. The chase was on my mind. I borrowed a truck and headed out. Not having driven for eight days and passing by the scene of the crash was eerie, and I was thankful when I turned onto the familiar dirt road. There is something about the rhythm of a dirt road maybe because you have to slow down, or perhaps the bumps lull you to ease. Peace began washing over me.

That time of year, this stretch of road is deserted save for an occasional big game hunter or dedicated angler. I arrived at my base camp, set up my teepee, and took out my binoculars to search the mountain for sheep. The sun was out, and I noticed a light breeze. Sure enough, I found a band of ewes and young rams on the mountains above. I spent the day playing cat and mouse with the sheep on steep terrain. There was not a ram I intended to shoot in the bunch, but I enjoyed practicing my approach. That night, I got back to camp with tired legs but in high spirits. For the first time, I felt more like myself, immersed in my surroundings. I cooked homemade deer sausage over the open fire and finished with a nightcap of Jameson. I do not remember anything from when my head hit the pillow until my alarm woke me the next morning. I had slept through the night, the first time since the accident. I am not sure why I slept so well that night. Maybe it was the exercise or the fresh air, maybe it was because I was hearing the wind rustle the aspens around my tent instead of the noises of the city. Regardless, I had finally found rest.

> *"There is something about the rhythm of a dirt road maybe because you have to slow down, or perhaps the bumps lull you to ease. Peace began washing over me."*

I felt renewed as I gathered myself, made breakfast, and searched the mountain for sheep. As the sun burned off the clouds, it revealed sheep nearby. Not seeing a mature ram though, I was content to go back home with more knowledge and a fresh mind. I had slept well and felt rejuvenated. I had hit reset on my nervous system and seemingly put the post-traumatic effects of the accident behind me. Upon returning home the reunion was grand. My wife could tell that I had turned a corner. I had found solace on the mountain.

That night back in my house, however, restlessness set in once more. The memory of the crash returned, and the following night brought more internal agitation. A foul mood set upon me, and I was not easy to be around. Again, the mountain was calling and I went. Nights were cooler up there, and before bed, I would start a fire on the stove in my teepee. The crackle of the fire, a calm mountain breeze, sounds of the river, and wind in the trees rocked me to sleep.

Throughout the ups and downs of this hunt, a clear pattern emerged. I was at peace in the woods and on the mountain and in turmoil back at home in my own bed. The contrast was undeniable. As time passed and the accident's intensity started to wane, I slowly began feeling safe at home again. Nevertheless, the out-of-doors continued to be the place that held the most solace for me.

That peace I had found on the mountain felt familiar. I thought back to another traumatic time in my life. I was nineteen, and my father had passed away. Acute leukemia took his life and created a deep hole, that still to this day has never been filled. A hole with glass edges that cut deep. During the hard weeks and months that followed his death, the only time I felt at peace was when I was in the woods or on the water. Maybe it is because I was so immersed in my surroundings, or maybe it was the natural rhythms of the wild that provide a place for me to heal. In nature, it seemed my father was always around the next bend in the river or over the next ridge. Over time the sharp edges of the hole have softened like glass on a beach but every once in a while I will come in touch with a sharp piece of raw emotions.

I wonder if Theodore Roosevelt felt similarly. His wife and mother had tragically died on the same day. The young Roosevelt, consumed with grief, headed west to amble across the prairies in pursuit of bison, elk, and pronghorn. While his mom and wife could never be replaced, he not only found peace on the prairie but also a desire to provide the same opportunities for all Americans. Before he left office, he set aside 240 million acres of public land for the best use, for the most people, for the greatest amount of time. I have been told this story for years by one of my beloved mentors, and without a doubt, it planted a seed in my own life.

With three days left in the sheep hunting season, I shot a beautiful, six-year-old bighorn ram. A sense of relief came over me as my hunt ended. My cousin had joined me that morning, and together we dined near the riverbank on fire-roasted sheep tenderloin as the sun set. A few feet away, a young moose sauntered across the river. I felt incredibly peaceful and noticed a sense of accomplishment for having endured. The mountain had provided me with sweet-tasting meat to share with friends and family, but more importantly, the mountain had provided me comfort and relief.

Today, when I feel the pressures of everyday life, a busy home life, airplane travel, or the coronavirus pandemic, I reset in the outdoors. Even if it is just a short walk around the block to feel the sun on my face, the breeze on my neck, or hear the sounds of the birds, it always brings me back to my center. Most of all, however, I feel taken care of by the mountain, a place that helps me find comfort, feel my father's presence, and heal from a traumatic experience.

Hunting: A Tradition of Silence, Solitude, and Being In Sync

Hunting is a tradition and heritage in which humans have engaged in since the beginning of our time on this planet. American outdoorsman and conservationist Steven Rinella says, "Maybe stalking the woods is as vital to the human condition as playing music or putting words to paper. Maybe hunting has as much of a claim on our civilized selves as anything else. After all, the earliest forms of representational art reflect hunters and prey. While the arts were making us spiritually viable, hunting did the heavy lifting of not only keeping us alive but inspiring us. To abhor hunting is to hate the place from which you came, which is akin to hating yourself in some distant, abstract way."

You may or may not feel drawn to hunting as it involves the intentional death of a non-domesticated animal. However, as hunting is an inherent part of the human story, you may want to consider the valuable components of this human custom.

Silence and Solitude

When in pursuit of most wild game, it matters not only where or when you are but how you are. Your manner dictates your success. Often you move silently and intentionally, being mindful of where you place each step, and always modifying the reaction of the life around you to your presence. When animals are near you, control your breath, your voice, your movements, and if the time comes, even your heart rate. The reality of hunting is that much of the time is meditative. Whether waiting for life to find you or perhaps searching for it, either way, patience is paramount while embracing the silence and solitude of a day in the woods, alone with nature.

Have you ever spent multiple hours outdoors in silence and solitude to blend in with the environment to encourage animals to show themselves?

Being in Sync

Hunting demands a certain understanding of the rhythm of nature. A hunter needs to be synced with the landscape. A shift in the wind, the phase of the moon, the tone of the birds–these are all important signs to the in-sync hunter.

Hunting is perhaps the ultimate communion with the outdoors. Hunters do not follow built trails nor do they only venture out when conditions are comfortable. Hunting is about following the breadcrumbs nature offers. Hunters know the feeling of watching the sun come up behind them and the forest come alive around them, not as they simply observe nature but truly partake in it.

Can you remember a time in which you truly felt in sync with nature all around you? What was that like? How do you orchestrate more in-sync moments like that?

Food for Thought

According to Aldo Leopold, "There are two spiritual dangers in not owning a farm. One is the danger of supposing that breakfast comes from the grocery store, and the other that heat comes from the furnace." Meat does not originate in the grocery store. It comes from the earth which supports the vegetation which rears the fauna that sustains us. The relationship between predator and prey is as old as life itself. Yet, as a society, we do not fully understand the impact of separating ourselves from the ancient tradition of hunting.

Do your food choices enhance or diminish your connection to the natural world?

Land Tawney

is a fifth-generation Montanan who developed his conservation ethic from a young age in duck blinds on warm water sloughs in the Bitterroot Valley, at the end of a fly rod during the salmon fly hatch on the Big Hole River, and chasing the wily wapiti in Cinnabar Basin. Land has spent his professional career building, energizing, and activating hunters and anglers to carry on our rich outdoor legacy. He currently is president and CEO of Backcountry Hunters & Anglers, the fastest-growing group of public lands advocates in North America. He lives in Missoula, Montana, with his wife Glenna, daughter Cidney, son Colin, and black Labrador retriever Tule.

IV.

NATURE AS SPIRITUAL GUIDE

Sacred Connections

Preface:
The psyche of a spiritually connected human race

"Nancy, can you tell me of a time in your life when you felt fully alive, a moment when time took on a curious quality, an instance where you felt part of something bigger? Some people may call this a spiritual experience." Nancy did not have to think about it for very long. Her eyes glazed over as she relayed the moment her beloved husband died after a long fight with cancer. "Barry suddenly woke from his terminal sleep as he took his last breath, and for the first time in months, he smiled at me, a tear running down the side of his cheek. It felt like I was on holy ground, the room was charged with a sudden spiritual current as Barry transitioned to the other side, his suffering replaced by an expression of peace." Nancy's moment of spiritual transcendence did not end here. As she left the hospice that day and arrived home, the rose bush Barry had planted for her was in full bloom, it was mid-April, a month ahead of its regular blooming schedule. As mystical as Nancy's story may seem, in my tenure at the Center for Grief and Loss, I encountered numerous accounts of deeply

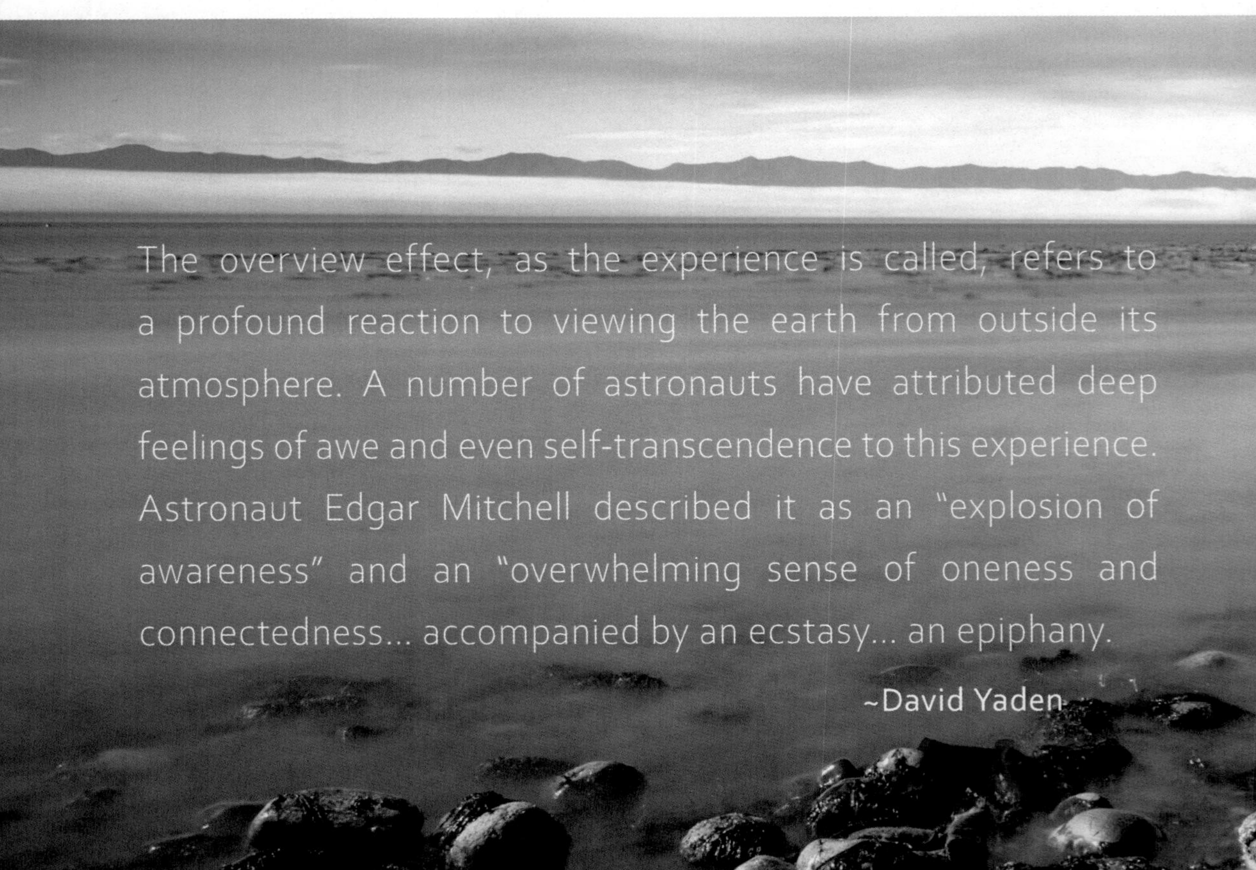

spiritual experiences, most of which arose from encounters with the natural world.

The spiritual connection between humans and nature is ancient and undeniable, like an invisible strand that ties us directly to the heartbeat of Mother Earth. There are windows in one's life, now and again, when we become aware of the connection, a joy fills our existence so intense that we lose all illusion of our superiority. For a few precious moments, we are moved from our sense of ego and separation to an eco-centric awareness of connection. We claim our birthright as a part of a greater whole, as part of an un-nameable, benevolent force.

What if the purpose of the spiritual journey is to uncover those moments? To put ourselves in the best possible environment to experience transcendence? We do not even have to travel to space or the Grand Canyon to encounter the strand. But we are more likely to discover spiritual connectedness in our garden than on our social media page.

When one thinks of the words "awe," "wonder," or "beauty," what images come to mind? If pictures of nature emerge, it is a clue that we are genuinely bonded to the forests, waters, and animals of our home planet. I believe that human survival is going to depend on a re-awakening to our place in the web of life and on a fortification of the strand that connects us back to the source of all life on earth.

Call of the Wild:
An exploration of interspecies sacredness

Dogs come into our lives to teach us about love. They depart to teach us about loss. A new dog never replaces an old dog, it merely expands the heart.

~Erica Jong

My first experience with the death of a loved one was when Casey, our devoted family dog, died after fifteen years. We named him after Casey Stengel, the playful former manager of the New York Yankees and Mets, and he often seemed intent on managing me, especially during his younger years when he slept beside my bed with a watchful eye. Sometimes he would jump up in the middle of the night, and I would awake to his warm body curled by my side.

We got Casey from a neighbor whose dog had puppies when I was five years old, and he became a constant companion during my developing years. I was tasked with taking him for walks to a park near our suburban New Jersey home, with him dragging me by a leash in his haste to get to wilder terrain. The park had a baseball field and playground adjacent to one of the few patches of woods in our sprawling community; most had been cut down for farms, but those were also disappearing, replaced by shopping malls, fast food joints, and prissy-named housing developments like "Willow Estates."

But the park was a haven, and Casey, our sweet, mid-sized, brown and white mutt, yearned to be set free. I knew what freedom might mean, but most times I let him off leash anyway to run in wide circles around the field as if a racehorse on a mission to win the Triple Crown. If he stopped and turned his gaze, looking at me, looking at the trees, I knew it could lead to an even faster dash into the heart of the woods. I would run after him yelling his name, but to no avail—some force, some magnetism had taken over, and he was gone. An hour or two later, he would return, barking outside the house, another force leading him home.

One Christmas Eve, he bolted into the woods to my great dismay and did not return in an hour or two. Many hours passed, and my worry increased, leading me to search for him in another patch of woods near a brown lake where we used to search for turtles and frogs and ice skated in the winter. I called his name in loud extended syllables, "Caaa-seeey!" But the only reply I got was from unseen neighborhood teens. "We ate him!" Followed by large laughs.

Keeping with my family's Scandinavian tradition, we shared gifts on the night before Christmas, and Casey always had a bone wrapped under the tree. Later in the evening, there was a knock on the door just before mom, dad, two older siblings and I were about to open presents despite our sadness over a missing family member. A friend had heard my calls, came across Casey, and wrangled him home by his collar, saving our celebration. My dad was initially in discipline mode, making him sit in the garage; but his howls and cries and whines penetrated the walls, and we were soon pleading for release. Dad, who wanted him with us as much as we did, relented and Casey quickly went from sad-eyed and remorseful to gleefully wagging his tail while chomping on his gift from Santa.

During my late teen years, with my energy peaking while his ebbed, our walks were far less vibrant. And when Casey suffered a stroke, and Dad took him to the vet, I did not realize he would not be coming home. I questioned my dad, but he said there was nothing they could do; the body and spirit that chased the wild were gone. I fought back tears, brooding over the eternal question of where life goes.

It was strange to not have a dog in the house after fifteen years of love and devotion and so many walks, but we did not get another, and I was soon off to college at nearby Rutgers and then for a try at graduate school at the University of Maine. Maine introduced me to the wilderness, and the graduate student couple I was staying with, Al and Judi, introduced me to their nearly two-hundred-pound, black Newfoundland, Mac, who became my closest companion.

Newfoundlands are amazing swimmers, with an instinct to save you if they think you are struggling in the water. We went swimming in the clear, cool Penobscot River, and Mac would paddle his huge paws toward me until I grabbed his tail and allowed him to drag me to shore. We performed the rescue mission over and over, and I thanked him every time. He seemed to love the ritual as if taking pleasure in helping a fellow being. Swimming and saving others was supposedly pure instinct, but I could not help feeling he was an old soul acting within some kind of awareness of the world soul or the life force that connects all things; at the least, Mac expressed a calming, yet vibrant emotional life.

One time, while walking along a forested path, Mac suddenly bolted left, off-trail and out of sight. I stopped, staring at the opening in the brush where he disappeared, and then called his name in a joking voice, "Hey Mac, where you goin'?" I always used a leash when we walked through town, but let him loose as soon as we hit the woods, although never telling Al and Judi, fearful that they would reject the idea. I did not think they would mind, but we were having so much fun with our freedom that I did not want to risk having it shut down. Minutes passed with no Mac in sight, and my joking tone turned to a nervous, "O-kaay, I may have lost Al and Judi's dog." My experiences with Casey told me that he could be gone for hours, and so I began calling Mac more seriously, and then with a touch of panic, wondering whether to follow his path through the woods or stay and keep hollering. Before I could decide, he burst through the brush and onto the trail—fifty yards ahead of me. If I had kept walking at our usual pace, I would have been at that exact spot.

"To saunter is to intentionally lose the world, along with our worries, returning to the roots of self and our place within nature, of which we are 'part and parcel.'"

When I caught up, his look seemed to say, "What were you doing back there?" It was a lesson in trust and the possibilities for nonverbal communication with nonhumans. Panic had caused me to fail to listen this time, but Mac and I had bonded in a language beyond words and thoughts, a language known by indigenous kinship cultures who practiced seeing the life force within all things, especially all things wild, as a lived reality.

The Maine woods and Mac lured me outside for daily walks, but I was also drawn to a book, Henry David Thoreau's Walden. I had never dipped into Thoreau's writings and thought my arrival in Maine signaled the right time. My initial interest began with an off-handed remark. I was chopping wood to earn a reduction in rent, turning red-faced from placing all my strength into the downward

thrust of an eight-pound maul. Al looked me over and laughed, "Chop your wood, and it warms you twice." It was the perfect remark, which he quickly attributed to Thoreau.

Thoreau, like Mac, felt like a kindred spirit, and I went on to read nearly all of his writings, including "Walking," his last essay before his early death from tuberculosis at age forty-four. My favorite high school books were Jack London's White Fang and The Call of the Wild, drawn in by the storytelling and bonds between dogs and humans, as well as London's exploration of the mysterious "wild," but Thoreau's essay gave me deeper insights into the absolute necessity for wilderness and wildness.

"Walking" explores sauntering, or walking as both a spiritual and radical act. To saunter is to intentionally lose the world, along with our worries, returning to the roots of self and our place within nature, of which we are "part and parcel." Thoreau, often the caustic critic but also humorous, remarked that he was surprised that his fellow townsfolk who busied themselves with business, forgetting what their legs are for, had not committed suicide long ago.

In "Walking," Thoreau made his famous claim: "In wildness is the preservation of the world." He witnessed encroaching industrialization and increased tameness in Concord and Boston, and sauntered west to find what was more wild and free, experiencing it as a healing tonic. Sauntering is spiritual because we often need to lose ourselves to find ourselves embedded within a wider world, and radical because such finding engenders responsibility, the call to listen beyond the human and to act.

Walking, in the manner of Thoreau, has become my daily practice. And these days, as an adult with my own family, my saunters are seldom alone. Snoopy, who came to us from our local Vermont animal shelter on my son's tenth birthday, is more like Casey than Mac, more mid-sized, rascally hound than a gentle giant, and he loves to run in the woods behind our house. Early mornings consist of Snoopy pacing the floor, looking at me expectantly, throwing in a whine, with me wanting coffee but often relenting to his instincts, which are also my instincts. In all seasons, the woods beckon, and Snoopy responds with unreserved leaps and bounds, trying to track the scent of a deer, or any fellow four-legged, any kind of wildness, which usually leads him to chase a squirrel up a tree. Sometimes a barred owl or woodpecker or crow can be heard, and then spied above. His hair raises, his tail shoots up, and his excitement overflows into what can only be described as pure ecstasy.

Snoopy joined our other dog, aging Rufus, who, while not quite as large as Mac, was even more gentle, in our clan of three kids, several chickens, and a bunny. Rufus was shipped to us from a shelter in Tennessee when our boys were toddlers. One morning, I awoke to a rumpled quilt without my wife's body, a pillow without her face. Confused, I reached for warmth, finding a nudge of the nose, then a paw lifted onto the bed. My wife was lying in the other room, a bad dream, a sniffle, the mother-love of a child having called her in, again, during the night to sleep with the boys in a row like puppies. What the hell, I thought, patting the edge of the bed. In a flash, Rufus was up, one hundred and twenty pounds of adoration affirming that we are all animals as we spooned to first light and birdsong.

Rufus was not a leap and bounder like Snoopy, more of a stay-relatively-close ambler. But, of course, he investigated everything in the woods, and while he got excited when greeting four-leggeds or two-leggeds, he most often seemed to practice equanimity, staying steady and true, lovable Rufus no matter the circumstance, including with young kids, who were leapers and bounders and fell all over him.

I cannot recall portraits of dogs in Thoreau's writings, as his focus was more on wild animals and wild places. He spent years surveying land to make a living, but loved unruly and intricate swamps far more than human-ordered landscapes, finding hope in their unfathomable aliveness—wetlands were jewels that dazzled with the force of life, saving us if we would have the foresight to save them. But the woods of Thoreau's time were cut down for farming and heating fuel—he wrote that he could seldom walk in the woods without hearing the chopping of an ax—and the worldwide wilderness, and the wildness it contains, is far tamer these days, dangerously tame. As a result, wildness, as a psychological state or experience, is so often dormant in us, but a good saunter in the woods, or a city park, or any patch of ground we can find, may bring us closer to doing what we can to preserve the world.

Despite domestication and taming, the wild still lived in Casey and Mac, and especially in Snoopy, despite his cartoon character name. A wild vigor lived in Rufus, too, but his back legs started to go after twelve years of devotion—him to us and us to him—and we eventually had to make the difficult decision of putting him down, at home and outside. We tried to prepare, but there was no preparation, only the trying that gives way to responding to the mystery of the other, the mystery of death, and the mystery of that moment. Rufus, in his soft black fur with white patches and big paw glory, was saint-like to us, responding to sadness by nuzzling with his big body and inviting eyes, wanting only to give and receive love.

After many tears—I have thankfully grown out of brooding and grown into the wisdom of gratitude and letting go—I have begun talking to Rufus in my head, and sometimes aloud, as our bonds change from mostly physical to something more. While the "something more" must be questioned and interpreted like everything else, seeing Rufus as a saint is not a mere projection but one description of how we met, or how he often met us, and what matters most is a continual interspecies, internatural, and inter-spiritual reaching out, learning more by being open to the wild and sacred within us and all things.

To Saunter As a Pilgrim

"I don't like either the word [hike] or the thing. People ought to saunter in the mountains – not 'hike!' Do you know the origin of that word saunter? It's a beautiful word. Away back in the middle ages people used to go on pilgrimages to the Holy Land, and when people in the villages through which they passed asked where they were going they would reply, 'A la sainte terre', 'To the Holy Land.' And so they became known as sainte-terre-ers or saunterers. Now these mountains are our Holy Land, and we ought to saunter through them reverently, not 'hike' through them."

~John Muir

Instructions for sauntering with your dog

Choosing a place to walk:

That one needs to decide on a place to walk seems obvious, but Thoreau was drawn to the West because in the early to mid-1800s, it was less developed and his instinct for wildness chose for him. For me, the wooded paths behind my house are the draw, but I sometimes let Snoopy choose which path, and I am rewarded with more unfamiliar terrain and a longer walk. Letting Snoopy choose also changes our relation from "owner/owned" to one that is more equal, more respectful, in which I can let go and not always be in charge—all good practices.

Processing thoughts:

To saunter is to leave the world behind, or rather, the weight of the world and our worries. Thoreau lamented walking miles in body but not getting there in mind and spirit, his thoughts remaining in the village. For him, we are not really sauntering until we have left worldly affairs behind, finding, of course, a much richer, much more diverse natural world. However, walks in the woods are also wonderful for processing thoughts and figuring things out about the world and ourselves, as the woods both enliven and allow the mind to rest and focus. Still, walking in the woods, especially with dogs who direct our attention away from ourselves, eventually takes us out of our heads, and thus out of our incessant ping-ponging between the past and the future.

Attending to our senses:

Dogs attend to their senses; we so often ignore ours. Thus, attending to our dog engenders our ability to attend to the senses. Follow their lead, observe what they observe, wonder about what they can smell and detect that we cannot, honor and mimic their excitement, their ecstasy in the created world. Attending to sense impressions directs us to the present moment, and, if we are lucky, we may experience synesthesia or the overlapping of senses that make us feel fully present and alive.

Following the call of the wild, inviting the spiritual:

For Thoreau, the wild is most alive and free, and that is why walking in the woods is a healing tonic. Body and mind are in sympathy and invigorated, but the call of the wild also elicits awareness of the spiritual. In Walden, Thoreau wrote, "Not till we are lost, in other words, not till we have lost the world, do we begin to find ourselves, and realize where we are and the infinite extent of our relations." Walking with dogs in the woods may start with processing thoughts of the world, then attending to our dogs and senses, deepening our relations with them, then to the diverse natural world and all our relations, with whom we are genetically kin but also spiritually connected via the mystery of life force, as well as the cycles of life and death.

Bringing our wild vigor and spiritual awareness back to the world:

We are not all fortunate to live near woods, or able to have dogs, yet walking as sauntering is a worthwhile practice wherever we live, including in cities. But if we can get a dog, hopefully from a shelter, or borrow one as I did with Mac, the wildness that remains within and without becomes more apparent and more honored, calling us in more life-giving ways. The sensuous and ecstatic voices of dogs remind me to listen beyond the human and then listen to my own voice, wild and spiritual, "refinding the compass," as Thoreau wrote, leading me to feel at home on this planet and inspired toward devotion and care. Thus, sauntering with canine companions is an education, and the learning that comes from returning to self and the world happens in steps, eliciting a profound openness to wildness, mystery, and the spiritual ground of a life well-lived.

William Homestead

is an associate professor in the Communication Studies department at New England College and has had a long association with the Ometeca Institute, a nonprofit devoted to the integration of sciences and humanities. His work with Ometeca, along with his interdisciplinary degrees (MA in Communication Studies, MS in Environmental Studies, MFA in Creative Writing), study with a spiritual teacher, and hiking experiences, provided much of the insight and inspiration for his book, An Ecology of Communication: Response and Responsibility in an Age of Ecocrisis. Homestead lives in Vermont and spends much time walking in the woods with his dog, Snoopy, who was named by his three children.

Conch Shell Calling:
On a mission to negate nature deprivation

People have this understanding that the natural world is equally accessible to all, but that is not the reality. For black individuals, it can be a fraught terrain where we are at the mercy of someone else's interpretation of our presence.

~Carolyn Finney

It was near perfect timing. I arrived just as the university shuttle bus came rolling onto Loyola's campus filled with excited eight- to twelve-year-olds from an outreach program in an economically depressed area of Baltimore City. The bus came to a stop in one of my favorite spots, no doubt the area responsible for the campus being known as Evergreen. The kids were full of energy as they lined up, impatient to get off the bus. As the door of the bus opened, the first child took one step down and stopped. With a big smile on my face, I welcomed him and extended my hand to help him down the next step. Rather than exit the bus, he stood there with his eyes and mouth wide open, almost frozen. The kids behind him were pushing each other and yelling for him to get off the bus. My hand still extended, I said, "It's okay; I can help you off the bus." After what seemed like an eternity with the other kids behind him still pushing and shoving each other to get off the bus, he softly said, "I have never ever seen this many trees in my whole life." I turned and looked at the stand of evergreens behind me, then just shy of being dismissive, I hurried him off the bus, so the other kids did not trample him or me. After getting off the bus, he stepped aside, and again said, "Wow, that is a whole lot of trees!"

Somewhat taken aback by his reaction, I asked if he wanted to walk down closer to the trees. With his friends calling out to him, he said, "No thanks," and ran to catch up with the others. But as I watched him run towards them, he kept looking back at the trees just like someone does who can hardly believe what he was seeing.

I was in no way oblivious to the trees, or the beauty of the entire campus for that matter. The first ten years of my career were spent working in Baltimore City, where concrete and tall buildings, not trees, predominated. While I loved my work, I was always so grateful at day's end to arrive home where I was enveloped by trees, grass, flowering shrubs, and all kinds of greenery.

Now here I was, working on a professionally landscaped college campus–beautiful every season of the year. Ironically, I worked in a windowless office, so seizing opportunities to be outside was one of my daily objectives. And that is how I ended up on this particular day, greeting the students as they got off the bus. I so vividly remember slowly walking back to my office trying to absorb what I had just experienced.

How a bank of trees could render such amazement to a child. Was that really the first time he had ever seen that many trees? Were there many others, children and

adults, who have never seen that many trees in one place? How might we share the beauty more broadly, particularly with those like that young boy? I became a woman on a mission.

The endeavor was not without its challenges, but the campus eventually joined in my efforts to have us be better stewards of our beautiful environs. Not surprisingly, one of the biggest hurdles was who we brought to campus. While bringing cute children of any color was not a big deal, bringing adults of color who "looked impoverished" was a huge hurdle. And so began the work of dismantling stereotypes. While that work continues today, the beautiful Evergreen Campus became much more hospitable, and children, women, and men of all ages, creeds, and colors were welcomed upon their arrival and always asked upon departure, how soon before they could come back. In large part, all because a little boy marveled at the trees on campus, someone noticed, reflected upon it, and was moved to action. There are days still when his reaction of awe and wonder gives me pause. In a way, it was similar to the reaction of a friend who I took on a kayaking trip.

My favorite place to connect with God involves water. Being near it or having a view of it is great, but being on it is a whole other experience. After one time in a kayak, I was hooked. Soon after discovering kayaking, I bought a boat, a single-seater rather than a double to preserve and maximize my peace on the water. One day, I invited my friend Geniece to go kayaking. She eventually accepted my invitation, I learned that day that she had no idea how to swim and feared the water. Still, she went. I remember the moment like it was yesterday, Geniece sitting in the still kayak in the narrow waterway amongst the tall reeds, the paddle lying horizontally across the open cockpit of the boat and her gazing upwards to the wide-open, beautiful, sunny, blue sky. It is a Kodak-of-the-heart moment forever etched in my memory.

Her demeanor was a far cry from the woman I had met many years earlier at an outreach center in Baltimore City, demanding that I find shelter for her and her four children for that night. Our kayaking outing highlighted how our relationship had evolved into a friendship. It was a gorgeous afternoon. Unloading the boats by the water's edge, Geniece suddenly got jittery. While reassuring her that the entire paddle would be in a very shallow area, I quickly moved into how to use the paddle. Next, I securely fitted her in the life vest. Very hesitantly, Geniece entered the boat, and ever so slowly I eased her boat into the water. Geniece immediately insisted I take the lead. Slowly, I led the way, turning back to check on her every sixty seconds. Though we mostly stayed close together, after

rounding one curve, I stopped to wait for Geniece. After what seemed like an unusually long time, I called her name several times. Hearing nothing, I mildly panicked and paddled back to look for her. As I rounded the bend, I saw her gazing up at the sky. I paddled up to her, "Geniece, are you okay?" "I have never, ever, in my whole life felt this much peace! Never!" she responded. I knew exactly what she meant. So many times, I had felt that same peace on the water, and I was so excited she, too, was having that experience. Together we sat there. Her expression radiated calm. Watching the experience of peace unfolding on the water, Anne Frank's words flooded my mind:

> *"The best remedy for those who are afraid, lonely or unhappy is to go outside, somewhere where they can be quiet, alone with the heavens, nature and God. Because only then does one feel that all is as it should be and that God wishes to see people happy, amidst the simple beauty of nature. I firmly believe that nature brings solace in all troubles."*

> *"I will always be grateful that our paths crossed, for all she taught me, and for having played a small part in her finding such peace that day on the water. Someday, I hope to recreate that experience for other[s] in Baltimore City."*

Geniece suffered an exceptionally hard life. Years of drug and alcohol abuse had ravaged her fragile body, mind, and spirit. Several months later, her body succumbed to all the abuse. I will always be grateful that our paths crossed, for all she taught me, and for having played a small part in her finding such peace that day on the water. Someday, I hope to recreate that experience for other Genieces in Baltimore City.

While much good resulted from the above stories–the young boy proclaiming, "I have never ever seen this many trees in my whole life!" and Geniece declaring, "I have never, ever in my whole life felt this much peace! Never!" I remain amazed by the amount of reflection those two experiences would elicit regarding my lifelong relationship with nature, and how it has developed through the years.

I was born and bred to be a nature lover and fortunate to grow up in a neighborhood that afforded me everything I needed to play in the outdoors: trees for swings and climbing, neighborhood streets safe for biking, hills for sledding, a pond for ice skating in the winter and for skimming stones for the rest of the year. For many years, I gave no thought to how being raised a nature lover shaped me. It has impacted my choice of a neighborhood, how I recreate, where I vacation, its effect on my imagination and dreams, who I spend time with, and most importantly my mental health and my spirituality. My most significant life decision was made one evening when I was "lost" in nature.

I had taken a few days off from work, mostly for some rest and relaxation and maybe some pondering on my next steps in life. I was staying at a place high above a body of water, off the beaten path, far from the lights of a town or city. During the day, I lingered for hours by the water's edge. In the dark of the evening, I wandered along a path through green fields.

One evening while walking, I was overtaken by the umbrella of stars and the radiance of the moon. Completely mesmerized by it all, I stopped and simply gazed upwards. Slowly, clouds began to appear. With the full moon luminous as ever, the clouds appeared to slowly pass behind it, never dulling the light of the moon. And almost out of nowhere it struck me this was God assuring me that s/he would always be with me, even in the midst of cloudy or uncertain times. It was a profound moment of assurance in which I felt God saying, "Have no fear!" Immediately following that moment, I began to feel confident about my future direction.

The next day, as I sat in an Adirondack chair high atop a hill looking down at the water still basking in the experience of the prior evening, I happened to glance to the rear of the arm of the chair. To my great surprise, there sat a conch shell. My immediate response was, "How'd that shell get here?" I didn't remember seeing it there when I sat down. With no one in sight who might have placed it there, I chose to believe that it was God and took it as further confirmation of the decision I had come to the night before.

This was not the first time God had placed a conch shell in my path, though it was the first time that it happened at such a distance from the water's edge. Thrilled to have decided my future, I was overwhelmed with peace and gratitude as the words of conservationist Rachel Carson echoed in my ears, "Those who contemplate the beauty of the earth find reserves of strength that will endure as long as life lasts." I left later that day, confident that I would always find the reserves of strength I needed to follow through on my decision.

I am deeply grateful for being attuned to nature from an early age and for discovering it to be my best, most trusted go-to place for discerning, decision-making, and recreating. I believe that the ways in which it has so positively shaped my life and wellbeing are immeasurable and feel secure in my well-established habits of accessing nature in the good, the challenging, and the uncertain times of my life. I continue to live haunted still by the realization that access to nature is an issue of privilege held by too few, and I remain committed to seeking ways to change that reality.

An Honest Look at Nature Privilege

The Center for American Progress states, "Nature is not an amenity but a necessity for everyone's health and well-being and that the long term negative impact of nature deprivation on a person's physical and mental health is nearly incalculable."

Candid reflections for personal exploration

- As a child was it generally safe for me to spend time outdoors?
- Did my parents or another adult figure mentor my relationship with nature?
- Can I name the identities that influence how I enter into relation with the natural world?
- How does my gender, age, geographic location, religious background, economic class, sexual identity, (dis)ability level, race, and ethnicity impact my connection with nature?
- Am I in the company of people of my race when recreating outdoors? How do people of different racial backgrounds answer this question?
- Are people of color widely represented in TV or magazine ads that cater to outdoor lovers?
- How can I or my community create inclusive spaces in nature?
- How do I create a sense of safety outdoors for friends who come from a marginalized community?

Catherine (Missy) Gugerty, SSND

is a passionate advocate for women, children and men experiencing homelessness and poverty. She began volunteering at an outreach center in Baltimore City while in high school and has made it her life's work. Immediately after college, Missy managed a small soup kitchen, moved on to manage Baltimore's largest meal program, was the Director of a men's shelter and employment program and later became the Director of the Center for Community Service and Justice at Loyola University Maryland. She currently serves on several non-profit boards. Missy holds a B.A. degree in Sociology and an M.S in Pastoral Counseling. She enjoys all things outdoors, loves introducing others to kayaking, nature photography and vacationing in Maine.

Hiking with Anger:

An invitation to authenticity

> I love to think of nature as an unlimited broadcasting station, through which God speaks to us every hour, if we will only tune in.
>
> ~George Washington Carver

It's the moments that add up to who we are. And it only takes a moment to change the trajectory of who you are becoming. It was such a moment in time that birthed darkness within the core of my being–darkness which led to the light. I could not have made this paradoxical pilgrimage without my spiritual guide–creation–gently awakening me to the beauty of Mary Oliver's wisdom, that this darkness, too, was a gift.

I spent my childhood among the trees; the forest and stream behind my house in Six Mile, South Carolina, were my companions. Hours of meditation (although I would not have known to name it this, nor would my faith tradition look kindly on this language) were spent with white pines, elms, and cedars while cold spring water nourished me. Creation's music soothed me. Wind and bird songs playing among the pines provided harmony. For me, the woods were my home–safe and welcoming. As a child, I knew deep in the core of my being that creation sustained my spirit. It is where I began to discover the authentic me.

If I am honest, the woods were the sanctuary that my family system could not provide; an escape from religious rules and family expectations. Selflessness, or literally "no-self," was the price in my family system for preserving the appearance of a healthy nuclear family. Any hint of disloyalty to this system brought shame, guilt, and–the worst punishment for me–the withdrawal of love, many times in the form of the "silent treatment."

"Come on, Greg, you know the family rules!" I was "a good little boy" and dissected myself from the authority I was being drawn toward. Even though no written "Cochran Family Contract" was signed, I knew the rules, all to create a public façade: "Those Cochrans, they have it together. What a perfect family with perfect children."

Still, somehow I believe because of an inherent Divine DNA and a few significant people who loved me toward wholeness, I was aware of a deeper, healthier conversation going on in the core of who I was. I have always heard this conversation most clearly when I was in nature's sanctuary.

One of those significant persons in my life was my Uncle Dwight. I was comfortable in his presence, whether it was being in his home, sitting around a fire while he and my other uncles played their guitars, eating at the Clock Diner listening to Willie Nelson and Waylon Jennings, or allowing me to make mistakes. He was always giving guidance instead of judgment.

The summer between my junior and senior year at Clemson University, my Uncle Dwight took me under his wings. Working for Southeastern Sprinkler Systems as his apprentice was hard, requiring early mornings and long days. Being with Uncle Dwight was worth it, though. I learned so much more than installing sprinkler systems: doing your best is all one can ask; making a mistake was an opportunity to learn; how to laugh; how to treat others with respect; about authenticity and many other life lessons.

> *"If I am honest, the woods were the sanctuary that my family system could not provide; an escape from religious rules and family expectations."*

But July 15, 1981 will forever be etched into the story of my life. We had just finished our lunch break. My uncle and I stepped back into the waist-high cage, and Terry, our co-worker, lifted us once again thirty feet into the rafters of the building where we were installing a sprinkler piping system. We had a rhythm to installing six-foot pieces of pipe running parallel between steel ceiling beams. Terry, driving the forklift that held the cage, would lower us enough to clear under a steel beam to the next bay where we would install the next pipe. It was well-rehearsed.

I do not know why–this question would haunt me if I would allow it–but at one point my uncle yelled down to Terry, "I believe we can make it to the next bay without you letting us down." For once, I did not emulate my uncle's actions. This would save my life. While he leaned over the top of the metal cage, I squatted down.

As we went under the next steel beam, my uncle became caught between the beam and the top of the cage. The next image that I can still vividly recall today was the unnatural, distant look within Uncle Dwight's eyes. In a panic, I yelled to Terry, "Drop the cage down!"I was hoping against hope that now there would be room for my uncle to breathe. Instead, he began to slump, go limp, and fall to the floor of the cage. Then his lifeless body began to slide through the open side of the steel rectangle where only moments ago we were talking and working. I dove and caught my uncle's legs as his limp torso hung over the edge of the cage floor, thirty feet in the air. As Terry continued to lower us to the warehouse floor, my mind and adrenals were racing, "Okay, Greg. He just passed out. He'll be okay. Others are coming to help. Just hang on, Greg." Reaching the ground, fellow construction workers had already rushed in, cradling my uncle's body and laying him gently on the cement floor where they started to administer CPR. It was too late. Uncle Dwight was not going to be okay. I remember the moment when I saw him take his last breath.

"I did not, I could not stop the strength behind two raging rivers, overwhelming and threatening, flowing counter to who I was taught to be and how life should be lived."

And with his last breath, I, too, became breathless. Darkness enveloped me. Who I thought I was, felt torn from me. All those religious and family rules I followed with loyalty, believed without question, and held as my safety and security, all of it was obliterated. I was lost in a free fall. The self I was discovering alongside my uncle died, too. My grounding had turned into shifting sand beneath my feet. And the pressure of a question was threatening to erupt: Why?

I do not remember much of my outward life for the next year. But inwardly, the ground was shaking. I did not, I could not stop the strength behind two raging rivers, overwhelming and threatening, flowing counter to who I was taught to be and how life should be lived. Two wild rivers: questions I was forbade to ask and anger I was supposed to deny. The force behind the rapids almost created too much anxiety to bear. How was I to know that these wild rivers would bring me home? Save my life?

In this wilderness, trying to hold the tension between the force of thundering rivers and the force of my childhood systems, I completed my senior year at

Clemson–although I do not remember much of that year. And as I neared graduation, still lost from myself, I decided to run away. I ran away from the questions and from simmering anger that was challenging what used to give me grounding. I ran from home and from my childhood constructs which now had cataclysmic cracks in what I once held as truth. This small-town boy ran away to the city. Of course, because it takes a long time to break away from a system, I ran away in the appropriate way. I escaped to a seminary in Louisville, Kentucky. What was I thinking? Deep down, my questions and anger were directed to whom I named God. I was not even sure there was a God. It was almost like I wanted to pick a fight. So, I went to God's turf. But in my running, I ran away–although not consciously–from where I felt most grounded, away from my truest sanctuary, the woods.

At seminary, I felt faithless. I could not find myself, or my place in the world. I forgot once again who I was. My old systems did not work for me any longer. And I could not remember that it was nature where I used to retreat, where I found solace, acceptance, and sanctuary, where I found my authentic self. I forgot that I knew who I was in the woods. For almost a decade, I set aside that pivotal knowledge.

I did not know it at the time, but my childhood companions–the trees, the streams–held a vigil for me. The wind and pines kept whispering my name. The rivers and birds continued to sing my songs, believing in me. Creation had not forgotten me. She tried to get through in simple, gentle ways. She blew softly on my face along the Ohio River in downtown Louisville. She embraced me within the endless Blue Ridge Mountains. She was giving life-saving breaths to my struggling soul just like those who shared their breath trying to save my uncle. Creation was waiting to lead me home to my authentic self.

One day, the therapist who was accompanying me through this dark period asked, "Have you ever taken an 'anger hike'?" As old tapes in my head played, my initial response was, "No, I don't get angry." Because that was the rule. Yet, I was intrigued and convinced myself to just go to a park, "You don't have to do an anger hike." I drove my canary yellow Volkswagen bug to Bernheim Forest near Louisville. For a while, I just sat at a secluded trailhead. But after some hesitation and self-talk, I did it. Feeling silly and guilty at first, I verbally stumbled to express what I had long denied– anger. As I started walking, however, my steps became quicker and more forceful, almost stomping. My "mad words" came more easily and were spoken from a deep, authentic place. I yelled at my mom, at my church, at God. I yelled the question, "Why?"

I had moved toward what I had feared would cost my personhood–my soul. I went back to my natural home, to my sanctuary, and I brought with me the forbidden taboos to let them loose. And Creation? She embraced me and said, "Welcome home, Greg," accepting all of who I was with no judgment. My trajectory shifted. I was in my sanctuary. Keenly aware of being grounded in something bigger than who I was, I heard the sound of the river. I smelled the leaf-carpeted forest. I heard the wind and trees playing. I woke up to the deep silence that was within all sounds. I was welcomed and accepted into a deeper conversation that was within me. I realized who I was. I was very aware that I was being saved–and still am.

It is the little moments that add up to who we are, that shepherd us into our authenticity. It only takes a moment to change the trajectory of who you are becoming. It was moments of trusting who I was in the woods as a child that would carry me through the dark moments I have experienced even until this day. Now when I walk, I try to pay attention within the moments, listening from my authentic self–discovered and nurtured by nature–to a deeper conversation taking place around and within me. Opening myself to learn more about who I am in relation to the greater Mystery of Creation, to others, and to myself, I feel grateful knowing the natural world calls me by name and continually reminds me of who I am.

Experiencing Creation as a Spiritual Guide

In reality, it is impossible to be truly present in every moment of our living. So give yourself a break. Still, the practice of being more open and aware of life's experiences can lead to more meaningful connections with self, others, Spirit, and the natural world–all moving us toward authenticity and wholeness. Here is an intentional way to welcome the moment and a deeper spiritual connection.

Take a "cathartic" hike

Whether by yourself or with a trusted friend, whether it is an "anger hike," "grief hike," or "celebratory hike," set your intentions to be aware of and open to a particular experience in your life, knowing all of Creation welcomes you into her caring, listening, and accepting heart.

Allow yourself to welcome the experience, thoughts, and feelings that stir within.

Rumi's poem, The Guest House, might be something you read as you set your intentions for your hike or as you stop along the way.

The Guest House
by Rumi

This being human is a guest house.
Every morning a new arrival.

A joy, a depression, a meanness,
some momentary awareness comes
as an unexpected visitor.

Welcome and entertain them all!
Even if they're a crowd of sorrows,
who violently sweep your house
empty of its furniture,
still, treat each guest honorably.
He may be clearing you out
for some new delight.

The dark thought, the shame, the malice,
meet them at the door laughing,
and invite them in.

Be grateful for whoever comes,
because each has been sent
as a guide from beyond.

Post hike reflections

Curiosity can be a more helpful attitude towards emotions than judgment.

- Did you become aware of a certain emotion present as you hiked? If yes, what emotion showed up?
- In what way did nature care for that emotion?

Mindful acceptance of emotions

Become curious about your experience. How do you feel emotionally? What kind of thoughts are going through your head? What does your body feel like at the moment?

- Watch your internal struggle without judging it.
- Feel the pain without drowning in it.
- Honor the hurt without becoming it.

Mindful acceptance is not about liking unpleasant feelings but about acknowledging them and no longer fighting or denying their presence.

"The meditator breathes in and says:
'Hello, my fear, my anger, my despair.
I will take good care of you."

Thich Nhat Hahn

Greg Cochran

is a spiritual companion and executive director at Well for the Journey in Lutherville, MD, adjunct staff for Shalem Institute's Spiritual Guidance Program in Washington, D.C., and for PASEO Spiritual Direction Program in Idaho and a minister. He is a woodworker, a photographer, a sojourner with and within Creation, a husband, dad, friend, and a fellow pilgrim in the world.

Towards a Wild God:
Facing mystery on the threshold

To be whole. To be complete. Wildness reminds us what it means to be human, what we are connected to rather than what we are separate from.

~Terry Tempest Williams

The last thing I expected was tears. I was on a solo overnight on the Black Forest Trail in North Central PA, enjoying the miracle of dusk at nine o'clock, and listening to the wood thrush still singing somewhere in the deep woods. Quite unexpectedly, I broke open. There was something in the absolute beauty of the birdsong, that late into the evening and that far into the woods that touched me deeply. I was feeling something more than gratitude, though, and could not seem to find a label for my emotion. I wandered over to a nearby ash tree, dead from disease, and I clung to it, so sad for its death, and found myself telling it how sorry I was that it had to die.

I remember looking up and being surprised by the crescent moon above the tree canopy. Everything, the birds, the trees, even the moon seemed so proximate as if together we had traveled to the edge of this wild, undefined, new place in me. I was unprepared for the journey, not able to trust what felt like a Holy Presence moving along the edges of the forest.

Lately, I had felt my relationship with God was changing. Growing up, I believed in God as a benevolent presence that loved me, often guided, and even protected me. But over the years, questions that had surfaced demanded attention. There was something not quite right about a God of certainties when the questions grew far outside the boundaries of absolutes. I found myself leaning more into a presence that invited me to simply sit with my uncertainty and to trust the journey of wonder more than the destination of truth.

On the trail that June night, I felt what was becoming a persistent tug in a new direction, towards a new relationship with what I now name Wild God.

> *"I found myself leaning more into a presence that invited me to simply sit with my uncertainty and to trust the journey of wonder more than the destination of truth."*

At one point, I remember calling out to the deep woods what felt like a ridiculous question even as I spoke the words into the air. Something like, "Is that you?"

I waited and listened until I felt a reply that centered deep within, sensing a smiling presence moving in and out of the trees, almost flirting with me from just beyond my small campsite. The presence was invitational, calling me to explore. Instead, I simply clung to the tree, lost in mystery, wanting to follow this Wild God and yet unable to let go.

I was facing a time of transformation in my own life's journey by initiating an intentional move away from my vocation as a local church pastor and into a role of wilderness guide of sorts, establishing an organization that would help people connect with God and with themselves through their encounters with nature. I had no script to follow and, without the structure of an organization behind me, I faced a surprising, new fear that I could not identify but I knew it had something to do with being alone, without the protection of a role to fill or a community to be a part of.

That night on the trail, I explored this fear as an invitation to a journey into an unfolding mystery connecting me with this Wild God. For centuries, people have embarked on outward journeys known as pilgrimages, sometimes in and through the wilderness to a sacred site. For me, this idea of pilgrimage became a journey within, to places in my heart that were fearsome to me. That evening in the woods was for me part of that holy walk into a new space and the silence of reawakening our souls to our sacred meant-for-ness. The archetypal framework for this journey is that the deep mountains opened a void that I had previously avoided.

In her ReWilding Wheel Workbook, Mary DeJong speaks to this idea of "getting up and moving to the parameters of our life, to the absolute edges, where we re-engage our senses and fully convey through the ancient practice of pilgrimage."

"My willingness to let go of certainty, to be open to trust, and to see vulnerability as a gift, leads to greater love, deeper understanding and acceptance, peace within, and possibilities for an authentic relationship with myself, with others, and with what I have come to know as God."

I feel as if I now stand on the edge of what I know, sensing an invitation to step over a threshold to experience what is waiting for me. The irony is that the openness, the surrender to silence through which I had been guiding others on retreats and backpacking trips, had never fully penetrated my soul until it surprised me that summer night. God had left the safe box of my creation and lured me into the wonderfully frightening possibilities of trust in the unknown mystery of a God that cannot be contained.

This experience led me to the wonderful and uncomfortable understanding that there is so much more. My willingness to let go of certainty, to be open to trust, and to see vulnerability as a gift, leads to greater love, deeper understanding and acceptance, peace within, and possibilities for an authentic relationship with myself, with others, and with what I have come to know as God.

What was it about that night, the deepening darkness of the forest, the mystery of the birdcall, the surprise of the crescent moon in the canopy? What was it in that moment that opened the first of what would be many doors? Perhaps my heart was ready, and the stillness of the evening, the sheer beauty of the birdsong, and the

warmth of the gentle breezes next to the creek helped to soften me. Deep in the wilderness, I found that facing the wild of the heart was more perplexing and dangerous than any solo trip into the woods. Maybe now I was finally ready to face some of the questions within and needed the prolonged space, silence, and stillness for them to finally emerge from underneath the layers.

Nature often surprises us at just the right time. Maybe our soul has been preparing for a season or a moment we didn't even realize would be crucial to our development as human beings. For me, it was an ongoing search that I did not realize was a part of me until I allowed myself the time and stillness to face the questions of faith and divinity in mystery rather than certainty.

More than a feeling, studies suggest that time spent in nature allows our brains to effectively mirror the slower pace of the forest. After some time settling into our surroundings in the wild, our brain's mirror neurons begin to match the slower pace of our surroundings: the treetops swaying high above in the canopy, a spider spinning a web, an ant crawling on a stem, ferns waving in the breeze. In the gift of slowing down, we find extraneous thoughts slipping away and creating room for a deeper connection with our inner selves.

Many gifts of nature help us to uncover what is unseen. My friend NashuWa is a member of the Passamaquoddy tribe in Northern Maine and a fellow forest therapy guide. NashuWa is a man with an amazing story who is living, in human terms, on 'borrowed time' after a traumatic brain injury. Through these past few years, he has learned and taught others about the gift of vulnerability to help dismantle the barriers to surrender and needed growth.

There is something about the beauty or the vastness of the wild that helps us to experience that vulnerability to be open to the possibilities that lie beyond our control. NashuWa tells a beautiful story from his own experience. One day several years ago, he walked into the woods intending to be small. He had learned to acknowledge the barriers that prevented him from truly seeing the world and his most authentic self, the inflated stuff of ego and power.

> *"In the gift of slowing down, we find extraneous thoughts slipping away and creating room for a deeper connection with our inner selves."*

He sat by a stream and closed his eyes, allowing the idea of smallness to pass through him and him through it. Time passed and NashuWa heard something very close in front of him. He slowly opened his eyes and there a doe stood in the stream, looking directly into the eyes of my friend. Again, he closed his eyes, focusing again on his smallness. More time passed, and after a while, NashuWa opened his eyes and looked upstream. He noticed something different about a stand of brown reeds just a few yards away. What was it? He looked and finally spotted an eye. The eye moved. A green heron, with his beak pointing straight into the air, had camouflaged himself among the reeds. This very intentional exercise continued to spill over into NashuWa's work with veterans and others searching for their place in a world that told them they were somehow unsuited for life as it had become. NashuWa can pass along this sacred teaching of beautiful vulnerability that eventually leads to strength in finding that we do indeed belong to the interwoven beauty of the world.

One of the gifts nature offers as an invitation out of that box of control is to be open and to step over a threshold within ourselves that we may not even realize is there. This sort of invitation is very different from setting out to conquer a mountain or testing ourselves against the elements. While there is a place for outward adventure in the wild, this sort of encounter with nature leads us on a journey inward. In some ways, it requires more courage than a test of physical ability. The journey inward can be fearful and necessary, and I realized it was one I'd been avoiding. After decades of leading others to truly slow and receive, I am just beginning to learn what that means for me. Nature leads and accompanies us in that process of slowing our bodies and our minds.

As a Nature and Forest Therapy guide, I lead groups on gentle walks in natural settings and throughout our time together I will issue various invitations designed to guide participants to a deeper interaction with the forest. On a weekend retreat last year, I invited a group of women to wander and simply find something that needed nurturing in the forest. One of the participants located a spot not too far away and sat for quite a while, leaning in the shade of an old pine, next to some young plants emerging from the forest floor. This woman, in her sixties, had dealt with crippling arthritis for most of her adult life, and her hands had become gnarled and very painful, making simple tasks difficult. When we returned to the circle for some conversation, this woman held her hands open on her lap and, visibly moved, began to share about her young granddaughter who had begun to question Betsy about her misshapen hands. She wondered, too, why her grandmother couldn't join her in the hands-on, rough, and tumble games she enjoyed. Betsy had been troubled by this and said she didn't realize the burden on her heart until she sat under the old, gnarled pine and recognized a kindred spirit. As she sat among the young plants near the base of the tree, she simultaneously grieved the loss and glimpsed the possibilities in many ways,

and her mind expanded to all the opportunities to shower her granddaughter with love, protection, and a nurturing presence as they grew and loved together.

> *"When I allow myself to be in wonderment of place, of wild beings, of self, I find an unexpected opening that invites me to a deeper journey of discovery."*

Professor and writer Belden Lane writes that "Backcountry, in its wild and unmanageable "otherness," takes you outside yourself and most deeply into yourself, only to find there a still more compelling wilderness." This is what Lane calls "A Spirituality of Wonderment" and maybe that is precisely where I am right now with the Wild God I think I'm trying to find. When I allow myself to be in wonderment of place, of wild beings, of self, I find an unexpected opening that invites me to a deeper journey of discovery. This 'unearthing' within often leads to healing, to a greater understanding of my most authentic self (without the ego getting in the way), or simply to a sense of peace in the next faithful step along the journey.

Connecting to the Source

"We are not humans on this earth seeking to have spiritual experiences; we are spirits having a human experience." ***-Pierre Teilhard de Chardin***

1. Wander outside in a natural setting, the woods, a park, or your own backyard until you find a place where you can pause for a while and simply be present.
2. Allow yourself some time to just breathe and perhaps focus on your breath as you let go of thoughts outside of this moment.
3. As you become more and more aware of your surroundings, allow yourself gratitude for a particular manifestation of life.
4. It may be a tree or birdsong, the pattern of water in a nearby stream, or the breezes bending the tips of the trees. As you notice and show gratitude, you may find your deeper self connecting with this source.
5. Give yourself some time to be in this presence. You may have a question to offer or you may discover feelings that you had avoided now coming to the surface. Allow whatever feels natural to rise in you and offer it to this presence.
6. Avoid placing expectations and instead allow yourself to be present and open. In returning to this practice, again and again, you may find yourself opening in new ways to a divine presence in the wild or within yourself, offering an invitation to something needed and new.

A Spiritual Examen

We take too few opportunities to ponder existential questions. A meaningful inquiry of what matters most can realign our lives to pursue a value-centered lifestyle. Read through these prompts and put your thoughts on paper.

Who/what do you put your hope in?

When have you felt most deeply and fully alive?

What legacy would you like to leave behind in your life?

From what sources, do you draw strength or courage?

Are there places or situations where you experience a divine presence more deeply?

As you look through your notes, do you notice a theme emerge? What role does nature play in your spiritual life?

Find an object in nature or think of a being from the more-than-human world that represents your spirituality. Keep a sketch or a photograph of that object in your home as a reminder of that spiritual connection and commit to a regular practice of nurturing.

Beth Jones

is the director of Deep Green Journey, an organization that helps create space in the wild to find healing, wholeness, and creativity. She is certified as a nature and forest therapy guide and leads backpacking excursions in the mountains of North Central Pennsylvania. An ordained pastor in the United Methodist Church, she has over 20 years of experience leading retreats and workshops and enjoys guiding groups to discover extraordinary possibilities in life, faith, and relationships through a restorative connection with the natural world.

Afterword:
Unplugging Generation Z

Almost everything will work again if you unplug it for a few minutes, including you.

~Anne Lamott

The internet is stressful; I am always waiting on an important text or email and I get anxious if I forget to check my notifications for even an hour or two. I was born in 1999 which qualifies me as a member of Generation Z, also known as the "Zoomers."

My generation is the first to grow up with portable electronics, unlimited internet access, and nonstop social media demands, a fact for which I am often grateful. I have been able to continue my college education and socialize with my friends amid a global pandemic because of the technological advancements of the 21st century. However, growing up with this abundance of technology does have downsides.

Many of my friends and classmates have become almost reliant on technology for entertainment and are out of touch with nature and their local environment as a result. Particularly in these times of self-isolation, it is easy to lose track of time and spend hours at a time looking at TikTok or YouTube videos without seeing the sunlight.

I was lucky to grow up in a family that cultivated an interest in the natural world, particularly through birding. Birding can take many forms – long mountain hikes, pelagic boat excursions, or just watching a feeder out the kitchen window – but my favorite way to bird is a springtime walk through the Eastern Deciduous Forest. At certain times of the year, Mid-Atlantic forests erupt in song and color. Even a brief walk through a wooded neighborhood can yield a startling number of beautiful songbirds – warblers, vireos, tanagers, and orioles, to name a few. During these few weeks in spring, the forests of the eastern US become akin to the tropical rainforests of the Amazon.

Several years ago, I introduced birding to my friend Zach. At a time when college stress began to wear on us both, Zach asked me to take him on some bird walks. Even though he had little knowledge and no experience, I could tell from our first walk that the activity resonated with him. He particularly appreciated how birding could help him achieve a state of mindfulness. Zach told me that diverting all your

attention to faint bird calls and methodically searching a wooded area for different birds helps bring about present moment awareness.

Birding isn't for everyone, there are other ways to get young people outside and engage in nature. For thrill-seekers like some of my college buddies, mountain biking, rock climbing, and slacklining are great options. These activities can be fun social experiences that allow you to appreciate nature while making friends and even improving physical fitness. For others, more calming choices include hiking or practicing art. In addition, while technology can be a stressor and unnecessary distraction, it can also be useful for familiarizing yourself with the local flora and fauna and connecting with the local natural community. The app iNaturalist can accurately identify species from the photos you capture on your phone. I spent hours during the beginning of lockdown walking around my neighborhood taking pictures of plants, insects, reptiles, and whatever else I could find in nature, or even just sitting and enjoying the scenery. Birding provides me with an excuse to put down my work, disconnect from my devices, and focus my senses entirely on locating and identifying whatever comes across my path.

I am committed to encouraging all young people to try and find an outdoor activity that resonates and connects them with nature. Unplug and find your birding or equivalent.

Max Rollfinke

is a graduate of the Davidson College Class of 2021 with a BS in Biology and a minor in Computer Science. He is pursuing a career in research related to Avian Ecology and Conservation and is taking several years to explore different field environments before potentially returning to school to attempt an MS. Max is currently stationed at Mattamuskeet NWR in North Carolina as a field technician on a study of the nesting ecology of Wood Ducks (Aix sponsa) and the contribution of manmade nest boxes to the breeding success of the species.

Acknowledgment

In ordinary life, we hardly realize that we receive a great deal more than we give and that it is only with gratitude that life becomes rich.

~Dietrich Bonhoeffer

First and foremost, I would like to acknowledge the invaluable contribution of every chapter author. Although each contribution tells a unique and significant story, the book in its entirety speaks so fondly of the human love story with the natural world. As we know the whole is greater than its parts. In that vein, each writer complemented this project in a profound way. I am ever grateful to all of you for letting the world hear a bit of your love story with Mother Nature.

Thank you to Dagmar Bohlman for sharing your knowledge and willingness to fine-comb through each person's story. You have dedicated time and creative energy to this project for which I am grateful.

Thank you to Franklin Adkinson for being an objective observer, providing valuable feedback when this project was still in its infancy.

My gratitude to Payton Schreiber-Pan for the countless hours of taking and editing photographs. Your meticulous efforts have made this book come alive with color and stunning nature imagery. When I decided to compile a book that showcases the natural world, it became obvious that a visual demonstration of human-nature-healing would be essential.

Appreciations to Sebastian Schreiber who agreed to use his creative talents to supply a few drawings for the book and his work on formating and typesetting.

Most importantly, thank you to my husband and confidant who is always supportive of my writing. It's been a beautiful experience to have nature be the cornerstone of our loving journey.

Dedication

To my father, Kurt, who taught me the love of nature.

12

References and Resources

Introduction & Preface - *Heidi Schreiber-Pan*

Resources:
Retreat Center in New Mexico www.vallecitos.org/

I.

I am Enough: The healing of self-doubt - *Dagmar Bohlmann*

References:

Ulrich, RS. View through a window may influence recovery from surgery. SCIENCE, 27 APR 1984 : 420-421.

Resources:

www.naturesacred.org

Heaviest Backpack: The space between dependence... - *Zoe Jack*

References:

Emerson, R. W. (1967). Self-reliance: An Essay. Mount Vernon, NY: Peter Pauper Press.

Ancestral Awakening: Finding myself... - *Laura Marques Brown*

References:

Roszak, T. E., Gomes, M. E., & Kanner, A. D. (1995). Ecopsychology: Restoring the earth, healing the mind. Sierra Club Books.

Williams, F. (2017). The nature fix: Why nature makes us happier, healthier, and more creative. WW Norton & Company.

Roz Katonah, MA APCC (www.seeds-of-awareness.org/essential_grid/roz-katonah-mft-trainee/)

Resources:
www.piscatawayindians.com

II.

Preface: Education of Homo Sapiens - *Heidi Schreiber-Pan*

References:

Heying, H., & Weinstein, B. (2021). A Hunter-gatherer's Guide to the 21st Century: Evolution and the Challenges of Modern Life. Penguin.

www.aacap.org/AACAP/Families_and_Youth/Facts_for_Families/FFF-Guide/Children-And-Watching-TV-054.aspx

Resources:

National Outdoor Leadership School www.nols.edu

Black or White: A zebra's lesson on identity - *Barney Wilson*

References:

De Cervantes, M. (2016). Don Quixote. Lulu. com.

World's Largest Zebra Crossing: The Famous Shibuya crossing www.youtube.com/watch?v=Od6EeCWytZo

Andrews, T. (2010). Animal speak: The spiritual & magical powers of creatures great and small. Llewellyn Worldwide.

Resources:

Advocating for Animals www.lindabender.org/

Ukulele Speaks: The power of music... - *Phillip McKnight*

Resources:

www.appalachiantrail.org/

Stretching for Growth: The perks of taking risks... - *Bryan Gomes*

References:

Nickerson, C. (2021). The Yerkes-Dodson Law and Performance. Simply Psychology.

Resources:

https://www.youtube.com/channel/UChLgI1GwWsKKEju9Vt8TPBA

Instagram: Chesapeakepearl

www.clearsharkh2o.org

Truth in the Saddle: Learning to show up - *Tracy Sanna*

References:

Jobe, T., Schultz-Jobe, B., & McFarland, L. (2016). Fundamentals of Natural Life manship: Trauma-Focused Equine Assisted Psychotherapy (TF-EAPTM). Liberty Hill: Natural Lifemanship, Texas, USA.

Louv, R. (2019). Our wild calling: How connecting with animals can transform our lives—and save theirs. Algonquin Books.

Perry, B. D., & Hambrick, E. P. (2008). The neurosequential model of therapeutics. Reclaiming children and youth, 17(3), 38-43.

Resouces:

www.naturallifemanship.com

www.eagala.org/index

III.

Preface: The emotional benefit of being... - *Heidi Schreiber-Pan*

References:

Muir, J. (1909). Our national parks. Houghton Mifflin.

David Attenborough Planet Earth BBC One www.bbc.co.uk/programmes/b006mywy

On Edge with Anxiety: A green heron leads... - *Brian Rollfinke*

Resources:

eBird www.eBird.org/home

iNaturalist www.inaturalist.org

Project FeederWatch www.feederwatch.org

A Blade of Grass: Freedom from addiction... - *Erin Quinley*

References:

Sambold, A. M. (2017). The Essential Rumi. Dispute Resolution Magazine, 24, 21.

Resources:

Substance Abuse and Mental Health Administration
1-800-662-4357 or www.samhsa.gov

Nature's Mothering: Walking together... - *Kate Gerwin*

Resources:

www.good-grief.org/goodgrief

www.griefshare.org

Hunting for Peace: A mountain helps... - *Land Tawney*

References:

Heller, P. (2012). The Dog Stars. Vintage.

Leopold, A. (1970). A sand county Almanac. 1949. New York: Ballantine.

Rinella, S. (2013). Meat eater: adventures from the life of an american hunter. Random House.

Resources:

www.adaa.org/understanding-anxiety/posttraumatic-stress-disorder-ptsd/resources

www.ptsd.va.gov

IV.

Preface: The psyche of a spiritually... - *Heidi Schreiber-Pan*

Resources:

The Science of Awe www.ggsc.berkeley.edu/images/uploads/GGSC-JTF_White_Paper-Awe_FINAL.pdf

Call of the Wild: An exploration of... - *William Homestead*

References:

Thoreau, H. D. (2012). Walden. The Portable Thoreau.

Thoreau, H. D., & Emerson, R. W. (1991). Nature/Walking. Intro. John Elder. Boston: Beacon P.

Resources:

www.thoreausociety.org/

The Wilderness Society www.wilderness.org

Conch Shell Calling: On a mission... - *Catherine (Missy) Gugerty*

Resources:

The Nature Gap - Center for American Progress www.americanprogress.org

The Children and Nature Network www.childrenandnature.org

Hiking with Anger: An invitation to authenticity - *Greg Cochran*

References:

Oliver, M. (2006). The uses of sorrow. Thirst. Boston: Beacon, 52.

Rumi, J. A. D., & Barks, C. (1995). The Essential Rumi (p. 414). Harmondsworth: Penguin.

Resources:

All Trails App www.alltrails.com/mobile

Towards a Wild God: Facing mystery on the threshold, Beth Jones

References:

DeJong, M.A. (2018). Rewilding Wheel Workbook. www.waymarkers.net/new-products/rewilding-wheel-workbook-1

Lane, B. C. (Ed.). (2014). Backpacking with the saints: Wilderness hiking as spiritual practice. Oxford University Press, USA.

Resources:

www.natureandforesttherapy.earth

~

Afterword: Unplugging Generation Z - *Max Rollfinke*

References:

iNaturalist App www.inaturalist.org/

Resources:

Birdwatching is the self-care we all need. Zach Jablow www.dbknews.com/2019/04/12/birdwatching-mindfulness-nature-environment-ornithology/

Contributors

Julie Ayers
www.salonz.wordpress.com

Dagmar Bohlmann
www.blissedbynature.com

Instagram: @blissed_by_nature

Facebook: @nature.blissed

Greg Cochran
Blog: Along the Way; www.gacochran.wordpress.com

Bryan Gomes
YouTube: www.youtube.com/channel/UChLgl1GwWsKKEju9Vt8TPBA

Facebook: Bryan Gomes ClearShark H20

www.clearsharkh2o.org

Catherine "Missy" Gugerty
Email: cgugerty@loyola.edu

William Homestead
Email: Whomestead@nec.edu

Beth Jones
www.deepgreenjourney.org

Laura Marques Brown
www.hopeignitedtraining.com/consultant/laura-marques-brown-she-her-ela/

www.anchoredhopetherapy.com/team/laura-marques-brown-lcpc/

Instagram: @anchoredhopetherapy

Phillip McKnight
www.cmhcweb.com/teams/phillip-mcknight-

Erin Quinley
Email: rinquin1@gmail.com

Brian Rollfinke
www.explorenature.org

Max Rollfinke
Instagram: @birdFinke

Tracy Sanna
tracysannacounseling.com

Gina Strauss
www.cmhcweb.com/teams/gina-strauss

Instagram: gina_strauss_professional

Land Tawney
www.backcountryhunters.org

Instagram: landtawney

Facebook: Land Tawney

Barney Wilson
LinkedIn: Dr. Barney J. Wilson

Email: barneywilson01@gmail.com

Credits

All **drawings** by **Sebastian Schreiber**

Photo page **42** courtesy of **Chelsea Haverly**

Photo page **56** courtesy of **Barney Wilson**

Photo page **99** courtesy of **Kristen Cooper**

Photos pages **101 and 169** courtesy of **Brian Rollfinke**

Photo page **121** courtesy of **Arne Wick**

Photos pages **134-139** courtesy of **William Homestead**

Photo page **158** courtesy of **Beth Jones**

All other photography including book jacket photos by Payton Schreiber-Pan

About the Editor

Heidi Schreiber-Pan, Ph.D. is a licensed professional clinical counselor and clinical director of the Chesapeake Mental Health Collaborative (CMHC) in Towson, Maryland, and founder of the newly launched Center for Nature-informed Therapy. Heidi specializes in the treatment of anxiety disorders, stress reduction, and occupational burnout from a nature-informed treatment lens.

Her workshops and seminars are offered all over the United States. As a former faculty member of Loyola University Maryland, her past research has focused on resiliency, psychological well-being, and nature-informed therapy.

She is the author of the successful self-help book: Taming the Anxious Mind.

For more information about the author, please go to:

www.heidischreiberpan.com

Made in the USA
Middletown, DE
21 April 2023